For the Love of

Afrim Pristine

For the Love of Cheese

Recipes and **Wisdom** from the

appetite
by RANDOM HOUSE

Appetite by Random House® and colophon are registered trademarks of Penguin Random House LLC.

Library and Archives of Canada Cataloguing in Publication is available upon request.

ISBN: 978-0-14-753046-2
eBook ISBN: 978-0-14-753047-9

Book design by CS Richardson
Photography by Steven Elphick, except for the following:
Ryan Faist: pp. iv, 180–181; courtesy of author: pp. 2–3, 4, 5, 6, 7, 8, 9, 90–91; Cindy La: p. x; Alexander Eidelman: pp. 33, 34, 69, 79, 87, 176, 194, 202; Jeffrey Chan: pp. 54, 111, 171; Ania Potyrala: p. 201; Johnny C.Y. Lam: p. 84.

Endpaper illustrations by Casey O'Neill
Illustration on p. 214 by Julio and Blair Lucas

Food styling by Julie Zambonelli

Printed and bound in China

Published in Canada by Appetite by Random House®
a division of Penguin Random House LLC.

www.penguinrandomhouse.ca

10 9 8 7 6 5 4 3 2 1

appetite
by RANDOM HOUSE

Penguin
Random House
Canada

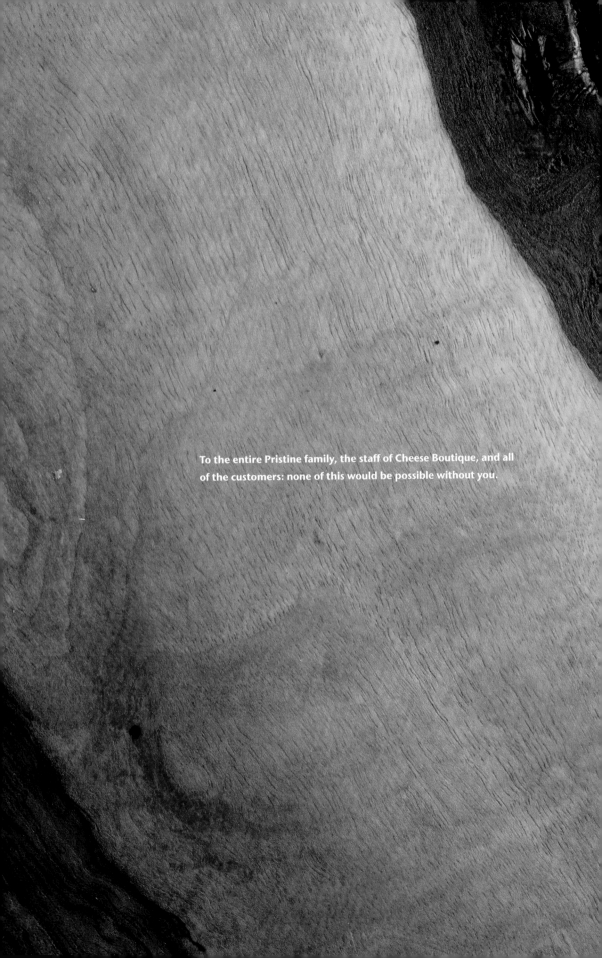

To the entire Pristine family, the staff of Cheese Boutique, and all of the customers: none of this would be possible without you.

1   Foreword by Michael Bonacini
5   Introduction

11   **Cheese 101**

21   **55 Cheeses**

35   **Breakfast**

53   **Lunch**

97   **Dinner**

137   **Dessert**

155   **Snacks**

177   **Low Risk, High Reward**

203   Acknowledgments
206   Index

Foreword by **Michael Bonacini**

I have often said that cheese is God's gift to chefs. But Afrim Pristine—well, he is God's gift to cheese! Not only is he generous with his encyclopedic knowledge, but his passion and appreciation for cheese knows no bounds.

I have come to know Afrim and his family slowly over the years. I would often shop at Cheese Boutique and see a young Afrim buzzing around the store, offering a slice of Manchego here or a taste of burrata there. His father, Fatos, might come over with a big copper tray of North African or Moroccan tea while his mom, Modesta, would pour a little Prosecco, and offer sausage rolls or cheese turnovers. Sometimes shopping there meant having a three-, four- or five-course lunch! It's clear that the Pristines are all larger-than-life individuals who truly love what they do. Running Cheese Boutique has been the center of their lives, culture, and dreams for years. When you visit the store, you are embraced by their genuine warmth and hospitality. And while Cheese Boutique's range of product, quality, and consistency are second to none, it's the Pristine family that makes it such a wonderful place to visit.

But there's no one quite like Afrim himself. An expert in his field, he never fails to regale you with a great story about a cheesemaker, or an interesting tidbit about the goats, cows, or sheep. He is not afraid to approach a table full of chefs or CEOs and wax poetic about a cheese's taste profile or aging process. It's incredible to hear someone speak so intelligently and passionately about food. His excitement is absolutely infectious and with this book, he'll be able to share that excitement with cheese-lovers worldwide. For too long, Afrim's recommendations have been limited to those lucky few who know him personally. In my experience, whether it's sourcing the perfect blue-veined cow's milk cheese for Auberge du Pommier's cheese cart, picking the squeakiest cheese curds for Bannock's poutine, or introducing the O&B team to a new type of cheese altogether, Afrim stays on top of his game. He travels far and wide to different dairies and farms, and brings that connection back to his customers—and now, to you, his readers.

As both a professional chef and a home cook who has enjoyed the expertise and warm hospitality of Afrim and Cheese Boutique for many years, it's so gratifying for me to see Afrim publish a cookbook all about his truest passion. I hope Afrim's lifelong love of cheese and this incredible collection of recipes will inspire you as it has me.

Michael Bonacini
Co-founder, Oliver & Bonacini Hospitality

Introduction

As I sit down to write this introduction and share a bit about myself with you, I can't help but wonder, how did a kid who almost failed out of ninth grade—who always preferred to be the class clown than the valedictorian—wind up here, writing a cookbook? It's a bit of a crazy feeling. But before I can tell you who I am and what I'm all about, we have to go back a few generations. Because the truth is that there's no way I'd be here if not for the hard work and dedication of those family members who came before me. Get your popcorn ready, people: this is going to be a fun, maybe bumpy, but super-tasty ride.

The Pristine family hails from all over Europe. My father, Fatos, and his family are of Albanian descent and my mother's family are of southern Italian descent. Both my parents grew up very poor. But they each had two loving parents, a strong sense of family, a love for food, and a work ethic that doesn't seem to exist in modern culture.

The 60s found my father traveling all over Europe—a hippie of sorts, but not the Grateful Dead type. Instead of cutting class and going to parties, my father read every book he could get his hands on and learned all about the vast and beautiful European cultures and cuisines surrounding him. He moved to Italy and began studying for his doctorate in political science at the University of Naples. And that's where he met Modesta Riccio and won the marriage lottery. My mom was studying for her doctorate in Latin at the same university. Their connection seemed meant to be—my mom grew up in the same tiny Italian town where my dad's mother had been born, Avellino. I always thought there must be something magical in the Avellino water, to have brought two such influential women into my dad's life.

While my parents were in school, falling in love, and presumably studying a bit too, my paternal grandparents, Stella and Hysen Pristine, were deciding what their next move should be. My grandfather was a strong, disciplined man, who had been involved in politics in Albania for much of his life. In the mid-60s, my grandparents saw many of their friends and colleagues emigrating from the Balkan countries and southern Europe to New York and Toronto. And though my grandparents hadn't been able to give my father as much as they would have liked, the decision they made to uproot their family and move to Toronto was the greatest gift they could have ever given him. As little as they had, Albania was still home for them, but once my father had finished

Hysen Pristine, my grandfather.

(Opposite) Dad, Agim and me at the store in 1997.

university, the Pristines packed up everything they could and, along with their four children (and my mom), moved to Toronto.

The arrival in Toronto was a bit of a cold awakening for my father. He took a job as a shipper and receiver for the Ponderosa Steakhouse restaurant chain. He packed and stacked skids of product. Meanwhile, my grandfather had gotten himself the opportunity to run a Becker's convenience store in the heart of Toronto's Bloor West Village. It seemed like the store would be a stepping stone to bigger and better things, and eventually it was. With their characteristic tenacity and strength of character, my grandfather and father put everything they had into their new lives. Soon, my father was working alongside my grandfather in the convenience store, selling Perrier (a novelty in the late 60s in Canada) and cigarettes to the community. In many ways, my family's success owes a lot to both those products—the customers kept coming back for both items, and the quick and easy cash flow allowed the Pristines to concentrate on some other areas of the business and plan for their goal of opening their very own store.

As the 60s came to a close, another opportunity came to my grandfather, and it was a big one.

A small, 600-square-foot space came up for rent just a few doors down from the convenience store. After some fierce negotiations, my grandfather and father signed a thirty-year lease. Every cent they'd saved, and every ounce of energy they had, went into opening something called "Cheese Boutique."

Why cheese, you ask? Seems an odd product to sell, especially for a powerful ex-politician from Albania and a doctor of political science. Simply put, my family decided to sell cheese because of that little old concept called "supply and demand."

Operating the old convenience store had sharpened my family's ability to discern what the customer wanted. Whether it was Perrier, cigarettes, or European products that reminded the community of their homelands, my family learned how to listen and subsequently deliver products from all over the world—all while offering a hospitable atmosphere. One of the products that we were constantly asked about was cheese. Even though we were a convenience store and not a full-scale supermarket, customers kept asking. So we gave it to them!

As the years passed, and the concept of Cheese Boutique grew more successful, my father started thinking of ways to expand our offerings. With whatever small amount of money he earned at Cheese Boutique, my father made regular weekend drives to Montreal, Quebec, to bring back beautiful, world-class cheeses

Hysen at the old store.

Dad, Hysen and Agim, 1990.

like authentic Brie de Meaux, farmhouse English cheddar, and Parmigiano-Reggiano. These cheeses were rarely distributed outside La Belle Province, but my dad kept at it, and his hard work paid off. The products started to fly off the shelf, the inventory got larger, and my family began to expand the selection of top-quality food offered at the store. Gorgeous breads, handmade sausages, unique jams and jellies, coffee, tea, pastries, and more all started appearing in the shop. If it was delicious and the best product available, my family wanted to sell it. At this time, the shop had become an even larger family business, with both my grandmother Stella and my uncle Fisnik helping out. Slowly, Cheese Boutique became a neighborhood anchor, but my father wanted more. He and my elegant, patient, loving mother wanted to start a family.

Four boys soon followed in close succession: Agim, Ilir, Afrim (yours truly), and Arian. My mother is an absolute saint. She stayed at home with us, trying to keep us all in line, which was not an easy task. My father worked his tail off, but always made time for his family—he'd call us every evening at 6 p.m. (an hour before the store technically closed) to speak to each of us, and ask what kind of treat we wanted from the shop (though he ignored my requests for Toblerone bars and instead just brought home cheese). To this day, I'm not sure how he and my mother did it.

In the 80s, the store expanded to the retail space next door as well, and my introduction to Cheese Boutique really began. I was eight years old, and working with the carpenters and woodworkers and of course Dad on the building of the new shop. I remember it as if it was yesterday: running around with sawdust on my pants, a hammer in my hand, and my Batman cape around my neck chasing my younger brother, who played the role of the Joker. Even at that early age, I knew that my family was building something special, that they were on a mission to shape how the city of Toronto ate. They wanted to leave their footprint on the city's culinary scene, and I wanted to be a part of it.

The new store on Ripley Ave, in 2000.

In 1991, my grandfather passed away. We were heartbroken to lose our patriarch. Hysen had done so much for the Albanian community in Toronto that to this day, I have customers who come in to retell their favorite stories of my grandfather. The responsibility of Cheese Boutique now fell solely on my father's shoulders, but my eldest brother, Agim, stepped up to assist. He was only a teenager, but he started spending more and more time at the shop and less time at school. Eventually, he dropped out of high school and went to work side by side with Dad. Of course, my highly academic parents weren't thrilled with this decision, but there was no changing my brother's mind. And I wasn't too far behind. I saw the sacrifices that my grandparents, parents, and brother had all made for the betterment of Cheese Boutique and, in turn, our family, and I realized that my turn was coming.

That turn presented itself on February 14, 1999. The night before, I had been out with friends and received a call late at night from my father to tell me that my brother Agim's wife, Sophia, was going into labor. Dad told me to meet him at the store at 6 a.m. the next morning so he could give me the keys. Then I had to open the store and stay there all day. It wasn't my first time working at Cheese Boutique, obviously, but this time would be different. I'd be the only Pristine on site, and on Valentine's Day moreover. That morning, as my dad quickly gave me the keys, he left with a few pieces of advice: "Be on the floor, be responsible, and make your family proud." That day, I flew around the store, bouncing from customer to customer, from the deli slicer to the cash register to the cheese counter. It was nothing different than my grandfather, father, or brother would have done, but I was so gratified knowing that I ran the shop on a busy holiday, and that our customers had walked away happy. Many hours later (Sophia had a tough, long labor), my beautiful niece, Ardiana, was born. The combination of a new Pristine baby and my father's pride in my work put me over the moon. At that moment, I knew that I wanted to continue to make him and the rest of my family proud. Cheese Boutique had given me so much, and now it was my time to give back to it.

The store continued to generate new and exciting opportunities for all of us. When my dad decided to move Cheese Boutique down the road a third time, to a huge warehouse nearby on Ripley Avenue, I was again reminded of the sacrifices that my family had made to ensure that this legacy would survive and benefit generations of Pristines to come. My parents put retirement aside and placed all their savings into the business—again—

Agim and I with Nizami Kolonari, a longtime employee and friend of my grandfather's.

My parents celebrating in Paris when Dad received the Chevalier Medal, 2004.

all to provide their children with bigger opportunities and the possibility of a better life than they had growing up.

And that's what we've been doing, these last twenty years. Dad sent me to Europe to learn from the best cheese makers and affineurs (people who age cheese) on the planet. I became a maître fromager—the world's youngest—in 2013, at the age of thirty-two. And since I've come back to Toronto, I've been learning from the greatest mentors possible—my dad and my brother—and have worked to try to make this family dream as great as it could be. Cheese in general and Cheese Boutique specifically have given me some pretty incredible experiences along the way too—visiting the famous cheese caves in Switzerland; having dinner one-on-one with perhaps the greatest chef ever born, Alain Ducasse; introducing one of my favorite bands (Weezer) onstage; writing this book, a true labor of love—none of it could have happened without Cheese Boutique and the love and support of the Cheese Boutique family and my own family. I hope that as you read and cook your way through these pages, that love will bring a smile to your face and joy to your palate.

Thank you for letting me share this with you,

Afrim

Construction of the new location on Ripley, 1998.

My Maître Fromager medal, 2013.

CHEESE 101

Here in Cheese 101, I'm going to break down everything you need to know about cheese—from buying it to storing it and enjoying it. Let's start at the beginning, with Mother Nature.

THE SEASONS

Perhaps the best part of cheese is its year-round availability. But, with that said, it's worth remembering that cheese is really just salt and fermented milk. When you change one of those two crucial ingredients, the final outcome can vary significantly. You might think to yourself that neither of these ingredients has anything to do with the seasons, but stay with me for a second. I have an equation that will blow your mind. Here goes:

> **Happy animals = happy milk =
> happy cheese**

Okay, I know, I might need to explain it a little differently.

Cows, goats, and sheep—the holy trinity of cheese-making animals—all love the same things. They love good food and good weather (and who the heck doesn't?). The goal for all dairy farmers and cheese makers is to give the best possible life to these animals. The happier the animals are, the better their milk will be, and the better their cheese will be.

Farmers want animals to roam the fields when the sun is shining, the grass is growing tall and full, and the flowers are blossoming. That beautiful summer grass, lush flowers, and bright herbs are so tasty for animals. And all of this translates into great-quality cheese. In the summer, animals' diets are steady and consistent; in the winter, they have to eat differently to accommodate the demands of that season. Just like humans, I find that animals want to tan, sip cocktails on patios, and take full advantage of the summer. In the winter, they—and we humans—mostly like to hibernate and snooze.

Knowing all this, let's get back to the cheese. I'm not saying that you can't make cheese in the winter, but you might not get the best out of the animals' milk in those stark, cold months. Don't believe me? Try an experiment for yourself. Go buy your favorite cheese in the summer months and try the exact same cheese in the dead of winter. I'm telling you, you will notice subtle differences. This difference is much more noticeable in youthful cheeses like fresh mozzarella or a younger brie, where the quality of the milk is very important to the taste. If a fresh mozzarella is only a few days old when you eat it, you're going to notice the quality of the milk.

You don't have to stop eating cheese in the winter, but be mindful that younger, fresher cheeses are best in the summer months. The fall and winter are for bigger, bolder aged cheeses. When a cheese is aged, that process becomes more important than the quality of the milk. Here's a good example: when a cheddar is five years old, the quality and simplicity of the milk take a back seat to issues like how the cheese was aged and cared for during that long, long time. What climate was created to age the cheese? What were the humidity levels in the cave? How often was the cheese tested for quality? All of these contribute to the aging process.

So, just as you think about vegetables having a season, think about cheese in the same way. In North America, you wouldn't expect tomatoes to be as delicious in January as they are in August. Instead of tomatoes, you look to winter vegetables like squashes and potatoes. Approach cheese that way too. If you're not sure about a cheese's season, ask your cheesemonger. They'll be more than happy to coach you through making the best choice for that time of year.

BUYING, STORING, AND AGING

The first thing I will tell you about this subject is simply: buy what you need. I've seen it too many times in my shop. Cheese lovers come in, and they get really excited by the aromas, textures and flavors of all the beautiful cheeses we carry. They eat with their eyes, and as much as the businessman inside me says "sell, sell, sell!" I try to refrain from letting my customers overbuy. The last thing I want is for the client to have a bad cheese experience. What's a bad cheese experience, you ask? I will explain.

Imagine that you go to your trusty cheese-monger, and you end up with much more cheese than you need. You just can't help it—you wanted it all! You arrive home overloaded with this goodness and put it away for when you're ready.

As I've said previously, many cheeses get better with age, but I'm not talking about the smaller, cut pieces that are wrapped up in your fridge. An amazing glass of wine, no matter how prized and rare, is meant to be drunk and enjoyed—you'd never think of saving a solitary glass of wine for later. And the same is true for cheese. A cut piece of cheese in your fridge isn't going to get better; rather, the opposite. And trust me, there is nothing worse than reaching into your fridge for your favorite cheese and dis-covering that it's way past its prime.

How should we remedy this? The answer is simple. Buy smaller pieces and visit your cheese-monger more frequently. Ask your cheesemon-ger questions such as:

- **What's really good today?**
- **What should I shave into my salad?**
- **What should I put onto my pasta?**
- **I'm having this wine with dinner tonight; what cheese would pair well with it?**

When you ask these kinds of questions, you'll get to know your cheesemonger. Develop a rela-tionship with them, get to know their schedule, get to know when the fresh buffalo mozzarella arrives, get to know who their favorite sports

*Authentic knife to
cut Swiss cheeses.*

team is, and more! Trying to establish a strong relationship with your cheesemonger might seem silly, but if you love great cheese, this connection will become incredibly valuable.

Now that you know how to buy your cheese, let's turn to storage. For the most part, if you're buying cheese from a reputable cheesemonger, you should keep the cheese in its original wax paper packaging. This wax paper is specially designed to store cheese. This will work for the first few days after you bring the cheese home. Beyond that point, you should rewrap the cheese in parchment paper and cover it tightly in aluminum foil. The cheese wax paper will only keep the moisture in for a few days; by covering it in fresh parchment paper followed by aluminum foil, you let the cheese breathe, without letting it dry out from being exposed to the air. This also works to keep the cheese from absorbing ambient scents or flavors in your fridge. And if you're a real cheese fiend like I am, you can dedicate your vegetable crisper as a cheese storage box. Who needs vegetables, anyway? Just remember to let the cheese come to room temperature completely before you serve it—you have to let the flavors open up, in much the same way as you decant a bottle of red wine. Depending on the cheese, this could take one to three hours. Promise me you won't serve it cold.

Lastly, in terms of aging, as you'll have read in the previous pages, much of the aging process will depend on the seasons. And every cheese is different. A freshly made mozzarella can and should be eaten as early as a few minutes old. Parmigiano-Reggiano, on the other hand, is typically aged for two to five years and some-times even longer. Is older cheese better? Not necessarily. It really depends on the particular cheese and, even more so, on your palate and preferences. When you age a cheese like Parmigiano-Reggiano, the flavors intensify—they get bigger, bolder, and sharper. Here is a general rule of thumb:

TYPE OF CHEESE	TYPICAL AGING PROCESS
FRESH (queso fresco, fresh mozzarella, burrata)	Up to **7 days**
SOFT (brie, camembert, fresh goat cheese)	**1 to 2 months**
SEMISOFT (Oka, havarti, Monterey Jack)	**3 to 6 months**
FIRM (Parmigiano-Reggiano, gouda, cheddar)	**3 to 6 years**

MILK TYPES

For such a simple food, cheese can be oh so complicated. As you now know, the quality of milk plays a hugely important role in the finished product. In Europe and North America—where 90 percent of the world's cheese comes from— milk from cows, goats, sheep, and, most recently, water buffalo dominates the cheese market. In other parts of the world, you'll sometimes see milk from yaks, moose, and donkeys being used to produce cheese.

For the purposes of this book, I'm going to stick to the basics and give you a rundown on the subtle differences between milk from cows, goats, sheep, and water buffalo.

Cow's milk tends to be the most neutral option, and you'll find that there are more varieties of cow's milk cheeses because there are simply more cows available for milking. The flavor is mild and delicate and can be used as a base for many further styles because of its relative neutrality— much more so than goat's and sheep's milks.

Goat's milk tends to be sour, acidic, and quite pungent. Even for the most passionate cheese fans, straight goat's milk may be too much. It has a unique flavor and often has a lush texture that coats your mouth. Goat's milk cheeses are eaten quite young and rarely aged longer than a few months.

Sheep's milk tends to be the most salty and tangy of all the milks. When you taste a nicely aged sheep cheese (six to twelve months), you can almost feel the salt on your taste buds. Bring on the red wine to wash all that goodness down.

Milk from water buffalo is the newest to the scene. Okay, I know, it's not actually that new, but it's super-hot right now to make cheese from it. Water buffalo can be found all over the world, and for many years, they were milked to produce cheese out of necessity—to feed the families who owned the animals. Today, one of the most popular cheeses being produced across the globe is fresh mozzarella di bufala. Don't confuse water buffalo with standard buffalo, though. Water buffalo are a specific breed of cow (and, fun fact, you cannot milk a traditional buffalo). This milk tends to be the richest yet most subtle of all the options described above; even in its simplicity, the flavor is full. This is why it's predominantly used to make fresh cheeses. It also has the highest milk fat content.

As modern cheese makers start to think outside the box, we're starting to see mixed-milk cheeses: half sheep's milk, half goat's; half goat's milk, half cow's. I find these new types of cheeses create umami explosions, and I urge you to try to hunt some down if you can.

Antique cheese probe from England.

PASTEURIZED VERSUS UNPASTEURIZED

I feel I should touch on this subject, even though it is a touchy one (pun intended, FYI).

You've learned that cheese is just milk and salt. And in the milk are natural bacteria. When you cook milk to a certain heat, you kill those bacteria, pasteurizing the milk.

Many cheese makers believe that unpasteurized cheese has superior flavor, but many government regulatory bodies feel otherwise. If you do some quick research, you'll see that there have been a few instances in the last fifty years where people have gotten sick and died from eating unpasteurized cheese. I want to stress that these occurrences have been very, very rare. Still, many governments have implemented something called the "sixty-day rule." In Canada and some US states, that rule dictates that we can produce and import unpasteurized cheese, but that the cheese must be aged and held at the dairy for the first sixty days of its life, as this is the highest-risk period (a low risk altogether, just to be clear). After the sixty days, the cheese can be sold on the open market. Other states have banned all production and importation of unpasteurized cheese, regardless of timing.

As all of you know, I'm not a doctor. I'm just a cheesemonger. I've heard many doctors say that pregnant women should steer clear of unpasteurized cheeses, because of the possibility of listeriosis. In Europe, especially France and Italy, where many unpasteurized cheeses are available, I've known many pregnant women (close family included) to eat them, and it's never been an issue. A few years ago, on a trip to the Loire Valley in France, I was having lunch beside two pregnant women who were just chowing down on the good stuff. Food for thought.

If you ask me, I don't think that unpasteurized milk makes better cheese than pasteurized milk—both are useful for different reasons. Unpasteurized cheeses are at their best when they are youthful

Cheese grater and planer from the Netherlands.

cheeses, because that's when the quality of the milk is so important. Fresh goat cheese and fresh mozzarella depend on those beautiful flavors, and shouldn't be aged. On the other hand, if a cheese is aged for two years or longer, it's not the quality of the milk that matters. The final product will depend on how that cheese has been aged and handled. If a dairy needs to hold the cheese for the first sixty days of its life, it won't make much difference to the consumer.

With all that said, I encourage you to do a bit more research on this if you like, as there are varying opinions on the subject. At the end of the day, you should make the decision that feels right for you.

THE CHEESE COURSE

Now that you know about the building blocks of cheese, it's time to bring it into your home in a major way. Not sure how to do that? Look to the Old World for inspiration! Every country in Europe eats and enjoys cheese differently. Here are a few examples.

In France and England, diners enjoy cheese at the end of the meal, with a great red wine left over from dinner. Cheese acts as a dessert, and these two countries take it to the next level. I've been in restaurants in France and England where the cheese trolley at the end of the meal is not just dessert but a culinary experience all on its own.

In Italy, where lunch is considered the most important meal of the day, a big block of cheese on the table is a common sight. As Italians enjoy a three-hour lunch with friends and family, that big block of cheese gets smaller and smaller throughout the meal. God bless the Italians—they are the only ones who eat cheese as a digestive. Eating cheese throughout the lunch allows you to eat more pasta, pizza, antipasto, etc. Italians also tend to cook with their cheeses—after all, pizza isn't pizza without mozzarella, and pasta isn't pasta without grated Parmigiano-Reggiano.

In the Netherlands, Germany, Austria, and many Scandinavian countries, cheese is often eaten in the morning for breakfast. Alongside delicious European high-milk-fat butter, flaky croissants, rustic bread, strong coffee, and fresh fruit, you'll find simple cheeses like Jarlsberg, butter cheese, and farmers' cheese. You simply cannot have a traditional breakfast without mild but flavorful cheese.

Although Greece is a fairly small country, its impact on the world of cheese has been huge. Halloumi and saganaki are both cheeses that are grilled or fried. And, of course, the Greeks have mastered feta. Feta has slowly become one of the most consumed cheeses in many Mediterranean cultures, and for good reason. Feta is usually served slightly chilled, for breakfast and lunch, with nice, ripe tomatoes, melons, olives, or seasonal vegetables. Where the climate is typically warm, feta can be quite refreshing in the heat.

Switzerland, much like Greece, is a small but significant contributor to European cheese. Classics like emmental, gruyère, and raclette are internationally beloved, especially for their melting properties. And when it comes to fondue, no one does it like the Swiss. Their cheeses on the whole are quite aromatic and stinky, and when melted, those flavors really open up. There's nothing better on a cold day or night than a rich, aromatic pot of cheese fondue, some crusty bread, cured meats, and all the other great fix-ings. Fondue is a huge part of Swiss culture, and you'll find it available at most times of the day.

In Spain and Portugal, where tapas cuisine is popular, cheese is traditionally seen in small-plate formats. You might find a dish of diced manchego cheese and quince paste, or a little anchovy and bell pepper canapé with a fresh goat's milk cheese. At the end of the day, both countries have cuisines that are highly ingredient focused, so they tend to keep it simple.

Of course, many more countries produce fantastic types of cheese, in Europe and beyond. In North America, we have diverse cultures and people who have immigrated from all over the world. And with that come diverse history, traditions, and cheese ideologies. We can enjoy tasty fromage at all times of the day, because all styles of cheeses are imported into North America, and we produce world-class cheese varieties of our own. The sky is really the limit.

THE PERFECT CHEESE PLATE

Now that you can picture the world on a plate, it's time to bring the global village to your own dining room with the perfect cheese plate. I've been asked about this topic a million times, and here is my answer once and for all.

When you're constructing your cheese platter, remember the word "contrast." The best part about cheese is the variety. All the flavors, aromas, and textures are amazing, and you want to hit each one of those and hit them differently. I like using five cheeses for my custom cheese plates. I also just love odd numbers, so seven is cool, too. But three ain't enough, so don't even try it. Here is what I would recommend, along with the appropriate fixings and garnishes:

- **a soft, creamy cow's milk cheese**
- **a soft or semisoft goat's milk cheese**
- **a firm or aged sheep's milk cheese**
- **a firm or aged cow's milk cheese**
- **a blue cheese, made from any milk**

This would be my ideal cheese plate in terms of the cheese selections, but if you follow these parameters even loosely, I don't think you can go wrong. If you don't like goat cheese, no problem: just switch it out for another flavor that contrasts with what you have already selected. The idea here is not to choose five different types of cheddars and throw them on your wooden board with some grapes. Let's put some thought into the selection, people! Have fun with it, and remember to try to appeal to various palates. Variety (in cheese) is the spice of life, after all.

Now, we need a few other ingredients to make the ultimate cheese board, but please remember, good cheese is and should always be the star of the show. Everything else is just detail, but let's make those details as good as they can be.

A few other goodies you want to have on hand are water-based and acidic fruits. Grapes, figs, apples, and pears are perfect to consume as you travel through the cheese board. They cleanse and refresh your palate so you can taste the beautiful, sometimes subtle, nuances of remarkable cheeses. I don't recommend fresh berries, as they have too much sugar content and tend to coat your palate rather than freshening it up.

You'll also want sweet and savory components. I love honeycomb, especially when it's in season. It pairs perfectly with salty cheese, like a big blue cheese. Good organic honey works well too. For the savory component, think about something like an onion chutney or pepper jelly for those stinky, ripe brie cheeses.

Crackers and breads are a must—they work as your vessel for the good stuff. I recommend fairly neutral flavors on this front, as you've already added lots of other components.

Nuts and dried fruit are your call. I don't personally love including either on my cheese board, as there are always allergies with nuts, and store-bought dried fruit typically contains sulphites, which can also cause allergic reactions. But again, that's a personal call.

Voilà! These simple rules are the key when it comes to the ultimate cheese board.

BOOZE AND CHEESE PAIRINGS

These cheeses are making me thirsty. Whether it's wine, beer, Scotch, or a fancy cocktail, there is always the right cheese for your drink. Are there rules? Of course not! It's your personal taste. So before you start reading this pairing section, please remember there are no rules to booze and cheese pairings. No one on the planet, no matter how acclaimed they are, can tell you what works and what doesn't work. I think pairings should be fun and suit whatever individual preferences you have. That said, I work with cheese for a living, so I wanted to share a few of my favorite booze and cheese pairings in the hopes that they will inspire you to create some of your own.

- **Aged creamy goat cheese and fresh acidic white wine. I love Valençay and a Sancerre white wine, both from the Loire Valley in France.**
- **Big, bold blue cheese and port or sherry. Try English stilton and a vintage tawny port.**
- **Aged cheddar and beer. Go for a robust lager and a five-year-old cheddar.**

Pairing alcohol and cheese is just like boxing. In boxing, a heavyweight fighter is always paired up against another heavyweight. A lightweight boxer is always paired up with another lightweight. Get what I'm saying here? You want the flavors to bounce off and play with each other—one shouldn't be more powerful. As long as you pair the cheese with alcohol of the same intensity, you'll get a knockout every time.

Cave-Aged
Gruyère

Brillat-Savarin

Burrata

Valdeon

Aged
Gouda

Oka

Manchego

Custom-Made
Parmigiano-Reggiano
Chisel

Parmigiano-
Reggiano

Cheese Curds

Valençay

Feta

My Top Ten Cheeses of All Time

I've been asked many times what my favorite cheese is. This is such an unfair question!
I have hundreds and hundreds of cheeses at my disposal, and you want me to just pick one?
I can offer you this, though. Once and for all, my top ten cheeses ever. I'll even put them in order.

1. PARMIGIANO-REGGIANO (Italy)
The king of cheeses, end of story.

2. VALENÇAY (France)
I adore cured Loire Valley goat cheese.

3. BURRATA (Italy)
There's nothing better than good tomatoes and fresh burrata in the summer.

4. YOUTHFUL MANCHEGO (Spain)
I always keep this in my fridge.

5. CAVE-AGED GRUYÈRE (Switzerland)
This is a nostalgic cheese for me, as visiting these caves was a highlight of my career.

6. AGED GOUDA (Netherlands)
This is for when you crave something to knock your socks off.

7. OKA (Canada)
Simple, straightforward, with the perfect amount of stink.

8. VALDEON (Spain)
When I crave blue, I want it to be big and powerful.

9. FETA (Greece)
Salty and delicious. Need I say more?

10. FRESH CHEESE CURDS (Canada)
Go, Canada, go!

Honorable mentions to: CHABICHOU, COMTÉ, CASHEL BLUE, BEEMSTER, BRIE DE MEAUX,
and—my mother will kill me if I skip this—fresh MOZZARELLA DI BUFALA.

55 CHEESES

THE CHEESE STANDS ALONE

On the following pages, you'll find a breakdown of each cheese used in my recipes.

NAME	**Boerenkaas**
COUNTRY	Netherlands
MILK	Cow (Pasteurized)
FLAVOR PROFILE	Tangy, buttery, rich
RECIPE	p. 36
FUN FACT	Beemster and gouda cheeses get all the fanfare in the Netherlands, but boerenkaas is really the star in my opinion.

NAME	**Monterey Jack**
COUNTRY	US
MILK	Cow (Pasteurized)
FLAVOR PROFILE	Buttery, mild, rich
RECIPE	p. 39
FUN FACT	For a long time, I didn't think much of Monterey Jack, but over the years, as I've started cooking more, I've realized that it's incredibly versatile.

NAME	**Cottage Cheese**
COUNTRY	US
MILK	Cow (Pasteurized)
FLAVOR PROFILE	Sweet, mild, light
RECIPE	p. 40
FUN FACT	Still not my fave, but it has its purposes. Who knew? Mild and bland can sometimes be good!

NAME	**Truffle Pecorino**
COUNTRY	Italy
MILK	Sheep (Pasteurized)
FLAVOR PROFILE	Earthy, mushroomy, salty
RECIPE	p. 43
FUN FACT	One of the most expensive cheeses in the world, but for good reason: it's fantastic.

NAME	**Santa Lucia Ricotta**
COUNTRY	Canada
MILK	Cow (Pasteurized)
FLAVOR PROFILE	Mild, light, creamy
RECIPE	p. 45
FUN FACT	A wicked ricotta, made by a wicked guy, Dominic Salvadore.

NAME	**Pecorino Fresco**
COUNTRY	Italy
MILK	Sheep (Pasteurized)
FLAVOR PROFILE	Sweet, fresh, unique aroma
RECIPE	p. 46
FUN FACT	In Tuscany, this is the most popular and often-used cheese in the summer.

NAME	**Queso Fresco**
COUNTRY	Mexico
MILK	Cow/goat (Pasteurized)
FLAVOR PROFILE	Creamy, soft, mild
RECIPE	p. 49
FUN FACT	Integral to the cuisine of Latin America, especially in Mexico.

NAME	**Wookey Hole Cheddar**
COUNTRY	UK
MILK	Cow (Pasteurized)
FLAVOR PROFILE	Nutty, sharp, full-bodied
RECIPE	p. 50
FUN FACT	One of the most famous cheddars in England, made in the Wookey Hole Caves. This is a cloth-bound cheddar.

NAME	**Feta**
COUNTRY	Greece
MILK	Goat (Pasteurized)
FLAVOR PROFILE	Salty, tangy, bold
RECIPES	pp. 56, 122
FUN FACT	Greece isn't the only country to produce great feta cheese. You'll often find feta in Macedonia, Turkey, Montenegro, Serbia, Croatia, Bulgaria, and Albania.

NAME	**Auricchio Provolone**
COUNTRY	Italy
MILK	Cow (Unpasteurized)
FLAVOR PROFILE	Bold, sharp, full-bodied
RECIPE	p. 126
FUN FACT	This cheese comes in all different shapes and sizes (most other cheeses are standardized sizes). In this case, size doesn't matter; it's delicious any way.

NAME	**Mozzarella di Bufala**
COUNTRY	Italy
MILK	Water buffalo (Pasteurized)
FLAVOR PROFILE	Fresh, mild, sweet
RECIPE	p. 60
FUN FACT	My father proposed to my mother on the Amalfi coast, while eating a mozzarella di bufala.

NAME	**Burrata**
COUNTRY	Italy
MILK	Water buffalo (Pasteurized)
FLAVOR PROFILE	Fresh, mild, sweet
RECIPE	p. 63
FUN FACT	This is one of the simplest eating cheeses there is, but it's one of the hardest to make.

NAME	**Zamorano**
COUNTRY	Spain
MILK	Sheep (Unpasteurized)
FLAVOR PROFILE	Buttery, nutty, salty, tangy
RECIPE	p. 64
FUN FACT	This cheese is manchego's bigger, bolder, louder brother.

NAME	**Halloumi**
COUNTRY	Cyprus
MILK	Goat/sheep (Pasteurized)
FLAVOR PROFILE	Salty, tangy, medium-bodied
RECIPE	pp. 71, 90
FUN FACT	Over the last two years, I've realized that I actually have an addiction to this cheese.

NAME	**Gouda**
COUNTRY	Netherlands
MILK	Cow (Pasteurized)
FLAVOR PROFILE	Fruity, buttery, medium-bodied
RECIPE	pp. 72, 169
FUN FACT	Be careful when you pronounce this cheese in front of someone Dutch. It should be said "how-duh," not "goo-da." The "g" has more of a guttural "h" sound in Dutch.

NAME	**Jarlsberg**
COUNTRY	Norway
MILK	Cow (Pasteurized)
FLAVOR PROFILE	Mild, buttery, sweet
RECIPE	pp. 75, 130
FUN FACT	This is the Swiss emmental of Scandinavia.

NAME	**Brie L'Extra**
COUNTRY	Canada
MILK	Cow (Pasteurized)
FLAVOR PROFILE	Fresh, mild, sweet
RECIPE	p. 76
FUN FACT	One of the best-selling brie-style cheeses in Canada.

NAME	**Ragusano**
COUNTRY	Italy
MILK	Cow (Pasteurized)
FLAVOR PROFILE	Savory, spicy, bold
RECIPES	pp. 78, 108
FUN FACT	I've discovered this cheese in the last ten years, and it doesn't get nearly enough fanfare.

NAME	**Valençay**
COUNTRY	France
MILK	Goat (Unpasteurized)
FLAVOR PROFILE	Citrusy, aromatic, medium-bodied
RECIPE	p. 80
FUN FACT	Another cheese I'm addicted to. The best producer, if you ask me, is Pierre Jacquin.

NAME	**Comté**
COUNTRY	France
MILK	Cow (Unpasteurized)
FLAVOR PROFILE	Nutty, fruity, medium-bodied
RECIPES	pp. 86, 183
FUN FACT	One of the greatest moments in my life was walking through the Comté caves with my father and the master cheese maker Jean-Charles Arnaud.

NAME	**Chabichou**
COUNTRY	France
MILK	Goat (Unpasteurized)
FLAVOR PROFILE	Fresh, creamy, aromatic
RECIPE	p. 178
FUN FACT	One of Charles de Gaulle's favorite cheeses.

NAME	**Glengarry Lankaaster**
COUNTRY	Canada
MILK	Cow (Pasteurized)
FLAVOR PROFILE	Buttery, nutty, medium-bodied
RECIPE	p. 92
FUN FACT	Produced two hours east of Toronto. Consistently one of the best cheeses made in Canada.

NAME	**Santa Lucia Cherry Bocconcini**
COUNTRY	Canada
MILK	Cow (Pasteurized)
FLAVOR PROFILE	Fresh, mild, sweet
RECIPE	p. 95
FUN FACT	These tasty little white globes elevate any salad.

NAME	**Oka**
COUNTRY	Canada
MILK	Cow (Pasteurized)
FLAVOR PROFILE	Aromatic, nutty, medium-bodied
RECIPE	p. 99
FUN FACT	This is one of the oldest cheese recipes in Canada. For many years, it was produced by monks.

NAME	**Oka L'Artisan**
COUNTRY	Canada
MILK	Cow (Pasteurized)
FLAVOR PROFILE	Aromatic, nutty, sharp
RECIPE	p. 100
FUN FACT	This newest Oka recipe is unique because of its honeycomb texture and aromatic flavor.

NAME	**Asiago**
COUNTRY	Italy
MILK	Cow (Pasteurized)
FLAVOR PROFILE	Sharp, salty, full-bodied
RECIPES	pp. 103, 105, 118
FUN FACT	Asiago is mother's milk to many northern Italians.

NAME	**Mascarpone**
COUNTRY	Italy
MILK	Cow (Pasteurized)
FLAVOR PROFILE	Buttery, creamy, mild, milky
RECIPES	pp. 104, 142, 144
FUN FACT	The beloved dessert tiramisu is nothing without the inclusion of this super-rich cheese.

NAME	**Grana Padano**
COUNTRY	Italy
MILK	Cow (Pasteurized)
FLAVOR PROFILE	Fruity, nutty, savory, sharp
RECIPE	p. 104
FUN FACT	It takes 1,000 liters of milk to produce one 90-pound wheel of Grana Padano.

NAME	**Swiss Raclette**
COUNTRY	Switzerland
MILK	Cow (Unpasteurized)
FLAVOR PROFILE	Stinky, sharp, full-bodied
RECIPE	p. 107
FUN FACT	Traditional raclette is delicious, but you can also find it with infusions of mustard, paprika, cognac, and peppercorns.

NAME	**Swiss Emmental**
COUNTRY	Switzerland
MILK	Cow (Unpasteurized)
FLAVOR PROFILE	Nutty, aromatic, sweet
RECIPES	pp. 82, 115, 196
FUN FACT	The original cheese in a "ham and cheese" sandwich. The holes in this cheese develop naturally from air pockets in the milk during production of the cheese.

NAME	**Swiss Gruyère**
COUNTRY	Switzerland
MILK	Cow (Unpasteurized)
FLAVOR PROFILE	Sharp, nutty, full-bodied
RECIPES	pp. 85, 112, 115, 132, 160
FUN FACT	The original cheese in a "croque monsieur" sand-wich. The name "gruyère" is protected like "Champagne."

NAME	**Parmigiano-Reggiano**
COUNTRY	Italy
MILK	Cow (Pasteurized)
FLAVOR PROFILE	Fruity, nutty, sharp, savory
RECIPES	pp. 66, 105, 110, 112, 151, 170
FUN FACT	The greatest of all time, the Muhammad Ali of cheese.

NAME	**Manchego Duero**
COUNTRY	Spain
MILK	Sheep (Pasteurized)
FLAVOR PROFILE	Fruity, nutty, sweet, tangy
RECIPE	p. 117
FUN FACT	It was Don Quixote who originally made this cheese famous—he and the cheese are both from La Mancha, Spain.

NAME	**Abbot's Gold Caramelised Onion Cheddar**
COUNTRY	UK
MILK	Cow (Pasteurized)
FLAVOR PROFILE	Mild, sweet, tangy
RECIPE	p. 121
FUN FACT	Made at the famous Wensleydale Creamery in Northern Yorkshire.

NAME	**Red Fox**
COUNTRY	UK
MILK	Cow (Pasteurized)
FLAVOR PROFILE	Nutty, sharp, medium-bodied
RECIPE	p. 125
FUN FACT	Produced at Belton Farm in Shropshire, England. The cheese gets its orange color from the addition of annatto seeds.

NAME	**Oaxaca**
COUNTRY	Mexico
MILK	Cow (Pasteurized)
FLAVOR PROFILE	Buttery, mild, salty
RECIPE	p. 129
FUN FACT	It's like mozzarella on steroids: bigger, bolder, creamier.

NAME	**Fontina**
COUNTRY	Italy
MILK	Cow (Unpasteurized)
FLAVOR PROFILE	Aromatic, strong, full-bodied
RECIPES	pp. 130, 134, 170
FUN FACT	Always try to find the real-deal Italian fontina made in the Valle D'Aosta.

NAME	**Brillat-Savarin**
COUNTRY	France
MILK	Cow (Pasteurized)
FLAVOR PROFILE	Buttery, nutty, sour
RECIPE	p. 138
FUN FACT	Made in honor of the first celebrity chef over a hundred years ago, Jean Anthelme Brillat-Savarin, a true pioneer.

NAME	**Chèvre des Alpes**
COUNTRY	Canada
MILK	Goat (Pasteurized)
FLAVOR PROFILE	Sour, fresh, acidic
RECIPE	p. 140
FUN FACT	This cheese is produced strictly from mountain goats.

NAME	**Roquefort Blue Cheese**
COUNTRY	France
MILK	Sheep (Unpasteurized)
FLAVOR PROFILE	Strong, salty, aromatic
RECIPE	p. 143
FUN FACT	The most important blue cheese ever created. No other blue really exists without this iconic touchstone.

NAME	**Cream Cheese**
COUNTRY	Canada & US
MILK	Cow (Pasteurized)
FLAVOR PROFILE	Creamy, mild, sweet
RECIPES	pp. 152, 168
FUN FACT	A bagel isn't complete without this cheese.

NAME	**Lemon Stilton**
COUNTRY	UK
MILK	Cow (Pasteurized)
FLAVOR PROFILE	Sweet, sour, fresh, acidic
RECIPE	p. 157
FUN FACT	On any given day, Cheese Boutique will stock fifteen to twenty different kinds of stilton cheese, lemon being just one.

NAME	**Havarti**
COUNTRY	US & Denmark
MILK	Cow (Pasteurized)
FLAVOR PROFILE	Buttery, rich, mild
RECIPE	p. 158
FUN FACT	This cheese is Denmark's pride and joy.

NAME	**Cotija**
COUNTRY	Mexico
MILK	Cow (Unpasteurized)
FLAVOR PROFILE	Salty, tangy, medium-bodied
RECIPE	p. 161
FUN FACT	The sky is the limit for uses of a good cotija.

NAME	**Appenzeller Swiss Cheese**
COUNTRY	Switzerland
MILK	Cow (Unpasteurized)
FLAVOR PROFILE	Nutty, sharp, strong, full-bodied
RECIPE	p. 164
FUN FACT	About seventy-five different dairies produce Appenzeller all over Switzerland—pretty impressive for such a small country.

NAME	**Mozzarella**
COUNTRY	Italy
MILK	Cow (Pasteurized)
FLAVOR PROFILE	Mild, smooth, light
RECIPES	pp. 108, 130, 173
FUN FACT	Perhaps the most recognized cheese ever made.

NAME	**Applewood Cheddar**
COUNTRY	UK
MILK	Cow (Pasteurized)
FLAVOR PROFILE	Smoky, sharp, full-bodied
RECIPE	p. 167
FUN FACT	Made by the Ilchester Cheese Company in Somerset, England. Arguably where some of the world's best cheddars originate.

NAME	**Prima Donna**
COUNTRY	Netherlands
MILK	Cow (Pasteurized)
FLAVOR PROFILE	Nutty, sweet, full-bodied
RECIPE	p. 174
FUN FACT	One of the most unfairly underrated cheeses ever. This stuff is delicious.

NAME	**Beemster**
COUNTRY	Netherlands
MILK	Cow (Pasteurized)
FLAVOR PROFILE	Sharp, nutty, caramel
RECIPE	p. 184
FUN FACT	Grate leftover bits of this tasty cheese and put it on your pasta. It's super-delicious and an umami explosion.

NAME	**Brie de Meaux**
COUNTRY	France
MILK	Cow (Unpasteurized)
FLAVOR PROFILE	Pungent, aromatic, sharp
RECIPE	p. 187
FUN FACT	Strictly speaking, brie can only be made in two French towns: Meaux and Melun.

NAME	**Pecorino Romano**
COUNTRY	Italy
MILK	Sheep (Pasteurized)
FLAVOR PROFILE	Salty, tangy, full-bodied
RECIPE	p. 188
FUN FACT	Produced all over southern Italy, but my favorite is made by Lupa Dairy in Sardinia.

NAME	**Cashel Blue**
COUNTRY	Ireland
MILK	Cow (Pasteurized)
FLAVOR PROFILE	Salty, aromatic, medium-bodied
RECIPE	p. 191
FUN FACT	This one is the holy grail of Irish cheese—it's a particular stand-out.

NAME	**Époisses**
COUNTRY	France
MILK	Cow (Pasteurized)
FLAVOR PROFILE	Pungent, strong, full-bodied
RECIPE	p. 195
FUN FACT	The most aggressive-smelling yet pleasant-tasting cheese you may ever come across. A true anomaly.

NAME	**Aged Auricchio Provolone**
COUNTRY	Italy
MILK	Cow (Unpasteurized)
FLAVOR PROFILE	Strong, bold, full-bodied
RECIPE	p. 200
FUN FACT	The Auricchio family is perhaps the most important cheese family in all of Italy.

Receiving the monster-sized provolone in 2006.

BREAKFAST

36 7 a.m. Pizza

39 Don't Mess with Texas Eggs

40 I Wish I Was at the Cottage Cheese Danish

43 Most Expensive Eggs Ever

45 Ricotta and Raspberry Sitting in a Tree . . .

46 Stefano's Pecorino Fresco Pancakes

49 Tortillas à la Marta

50 Wookey and Waffles

7 a.m. Pizza

PREP 15 minutes
COOK 25–30 minutes
SERVES 2–4

1 lb (450 g) ground breakfast sausage
Splash of olive oil
1 package (8 oz/225 g) crescent roll dough
1 cup (250 ml) frozen hash brown potatoes, thawed
1 cup (250 ml) shredded boerenkaas cheese
4 medium eggs
¼ cup (60 ml) 2% milk
½ tsp (2 ml) sea salt
¼ tsp (1 ml) ground pepper

1. Preheat the oven to 375°F (190°C).
2. In a medium-sized deep skillet, combine the sausage with a splash of olive oil and set over medium-high heat. Cook for 4 to 5 minutes or until evenly browned. Drain, crumble, and set aside at room temperature.
3. Separate the crescent roll dough into 8 triangular pieces. Place them on an ungreased 12-inch (30 cm) pizza pan with the longest sides pointing toward the center of the pan. Press the triangles together to form a crust. The bottom of the crust should be sealed and the outside edge should be slightly raised.
4. Spoon the browned sausage over the crust. Sprinkle with the hash browns, and top with the boerenkaas cheese.
5. In a small bowl, beat the eggs together. Add the milk, and finish with the salt and pepper. Mix well, then evenly pour the egg mixture over the pizza. Go slowly!
6. Bake the pizza for 25 to 30 minutes or until the eggs are set, and serve in slices.

CHEESE:
Boerenkaas

For this recipe, boerenkaas cheese works well because it melts so perfectly. If boerenkaas had children, they'd be named Ooey and Gooey. If you have the time, make fresh pizza dough instead of using the crescent rolls. Check out a simple and wicked pizza dough recipe by Chef Rocco Agostino (page 113).

Tom McLean made this beautiful knife for me. Thanks Tom!

If the Dallas Cowboys is America's team, then Monterey Jack is America's cheese. You'll find it all over North America, and although it's simple, it has some great qualities. Its mild flavor and gooey texture will never overpower a dish, and it can take a burger or nachos to the next level.

Don't Mess with Texas Eggs

PREP	15 minutes
COOK	20 minutes
SERVES	The entire defensive line of the Dallas Cowboys or 6 hungry people

½ medium red bell pepper
½ medium yellow bell pepper
½ medium green bell pepper
2 Tbsp (30 ml) unsalted butter
1 medium white onion, finely chopped
2 cloves garlic, finely chopped
1 can (19 oz/540 ml) white kidney beans, rinsed and drained
4 medium plum tomatoes, thinly sliced
1 tsp (5 ml) chili powder
2½ cups (625 ml) good-quality tomato sauce
Sea salt and freshly ground pepper
6 large eggs
6 oz (170 g) Monterey Jack cheese, shredded
Crusty bread, for serving

1. Preheat the oven to 450°F (230°C).
2. Cut the 3 types of bell peppers into strips lengthwise.
3. In a 12-inch (30 cm) oven-safe skillet, melt the butter over medium heat. Sauté the onion, garlic, and white kidney beans for approximately 5 minutes or until softened and starting to caramelize. Add the bell peppers, tomatoes, and chili powder. Cook for an additional 5 minutes. Pour the tomato sauce into the skillet, stir well, and bring to a boil. Season to taste with salt and pepper.
4. Spacing them evenly around the skillet, crack the eggs, 1 at a time, into the skillet. Do not stir. Top the mixture with Monterey Jack cheese, and place in the preheated oven. Bake for 3 to 4 minutes or until the cheese is golden brown.
5. Scoop the eggs and tomato sauce onto serving plates, and serve immediately with crusty bread.

I Wish I Was at the Cottage
Cheese Danish

CHEESE:
Cottage

PREP	15 minutes
COOK	20–25 minutes
SERVES	6

8 oz (225 g) drained cottage cheese (see note)

⅓ cup + 2 tsp (95 ml) granulated sugar, divided

1 large egg

1 tsp (5 ml) vanilla extract

¼ tsp (1 ml) fine sea salt

2 medium royal gala apples (or another apple you enjoy), thinly
   sliced

1 tsp (5 ml) lemon juice

1 sheet store-bought puff pastry, thawed

Icing sugar, for sprinkling

½ tsp (2 ml) cinnamon (optional)

1. Preheat the oven to 400°F (200°C), and line a baking sheet
   with parchment paper.
2. In a medium bowl, combine the cottage cheese, ⅓ cup
   (85 mL) sugar, egg, vanilla, and salt. Mix well, and set aside at
   room temperature.
3. In a small bowl, toss the sliced apples with the lemon juice
   and remaining 2 teaspoons (10 ml) of sugar. Set aside at room
   temperature.
4. Using a pizza cutter, cut the thawed puff pastry lengthwise into
   six 6-inch (15 cm) squares. Divide the cheese mixture among the
   squares, and top with the sliced apples. Fold in the 2 opposite
   corners of each dough square to meet in the middle of the
   pastry, then pinch them together. Pinch the edges of the pastry
   together, but leave some room at the end for steam to escape.
   Sprinkle with icing sugar and cinnamon, and place the
   Danishes onto the prepared baking sheet.
5. Bake the Danishes for 20 to 25 minutes or until golden brown.
6. Enjoy at least 1 Danish fresh out of the oven, and let the rest
   cool on the counter. Transfer the Danishes to an airtight
   container. They will keep on the counter for up to 2 days.

If anyone tells you they like to eat cottage cheese on its own, without anything else with it, they are lying. Trust me. Honestly, there isn't much to cottage cheese, although it's great to bake with. It's a very fresh cow's milk cheese with the excess milk drained out. It's mushy in texture and mild in flavor (are you hungry yet?). I want to show cottage cheese some love, so this recipe is incredibly easy and is a fantastic way to use this kind of cheese.

Just like with all cheeses, the higher the milk fat percentage, the tastier the product. Try to find 8% fat cottage cheese, if you can.

CHEESE:
Truffle
Pecorino

Most Expensive Eggs Ever

PREP	A really long minute
COOK	3 minutes
SERVES	1 hungry human being

⅓ cup (85 ml) grated truffle pecorino cheese
2 large eggs
Freshly ground pepper (see note)

1. Place the pecorino cheese in a medium skillet over high heat (no butter or oil needed, just watch). As the cheese starts melting, it will release its natural oils. Crack the eggs on top of the cheese. Season to taste with pepper, and resist the temptation to lick the walls because your kitchen smells so good. Cook the eggs for approximately 3 minutes or until the whites are set (or to your personal preference). No need to stir; just allow them to cook as is.

2. Scoop and serve!

Truffle pecorino is a cheese that combines 2 powerhouse ingredients: delicious pecorino cheese (see page 188 to learn more about pecorino cheese) and fresh black truffles. When you go to your local cheesemonger, see what they have and ask for a taste. What you are looking for is that sharp, sheep-like taste from the cheese and the aromatics from the truffle. This cheese isn't cheap, but it's a perfect treat, and when you pair it with hearty farm-fresh eggs, you get a star-studded combo, like Sonny and Cher, Starsky and Hutch, Bert and Ernie, and, of course, Batman and Robin (except for when Chris O'Donnell played Robin, because that was just terrible).

No salt is needed in this recipe as the cheese is salty enough and will naturally season the eggs. If you really want to splurge, you can put freshly shaved black truffles on top of the cheesy eggs. But that's your call.

If you put gin or vodka in it,
I won't tell anyone. Enjoy!

Ricotta and Raspberry Sitting in a Tree . . .

PREP	5 minutes
COOK	None
SERVES	Me, myself, and I

¼ cup (60 ml) Santa Lucia ricotta cheese

¾ cup (185 ml) 2% milk

1½ cups (375 ml) frozen raspberries

1½ Tbsp (25 ml) wildflower honey

½ tsp (2 ml) vanilla extract

1. Throw all the ingredients into a blender. Blend the daylights out of everything.

The Italians struck dairy gold when the simple, sweet ricotta was born. I use ricotta in a few different recipes (see pages 66, 140, 142, and 168) but this next one is the perfect way to start your day. I know that not many of us have the time to sit down and enjoy breakfast (at least, those of us not living in Europe), but this recipe is quick, healthy, and satisfying. Pair it with a double shot of espresso and you'll be ready to go hard for a 13-hour shift, just like me.

Stefano's Pecorino Fresco
Pancakes

PREP	10 minutes
COOK	12 minutes
SERVES	2

⅓ cup (85 ml) all-purpose flour

⅔ cup (165 ml) whole wheat flour

1 tsp (5 ml) baking powder

½ tsp (2 ml) baking soda

¼ cup (60 ml) sugar

1 tsp (5 ml) ground cinnamon

½ tsp (2 ml) ground nutmeg

¼ tsp (1 ml) ground ginger

1 large egg

1 cup (250 ml) whole milk

½ cup (125 ml) finely shredded pecorino fresco cheese

1 tsp (5 ml) vanilla extract

1–2 Tbsp (15–30 ml) unsalted butter

1. Preheat the oven to 200°F (95°C).
2. In a large bowl, mix together both flours, baking powder, baking soda, sugar, cinnamon, nutmeg, and ginger. Make a well in the center of the mixture, and set aside at room temperature.
3. In a medium bowl, beat the egg with the milk. Add the pecorino fresco cheese and vanilla. Mix well. Pour the wet ingredients into the well of the dry ingredients bowl. Whisk until combined.
4. In a medium skillet, melt the butter over medium heat. Using a ⅓-cup measure, scoop out some of the batter and place it in the pan. Cook for approximately 2 minutes per side or until golden brown. Transfer the pancakes to a baking sheet and keep them warm in the oven until you're ready to eat them. Repeat with the remaining batter, adding more butter if needed.
5. You can dress up the pancakes with maple syrup, jelly, or butter. Serve hot!

Il Forteto Dairy is situated in the small town of Vicchio in Tuscany. I spent a few weeks there in 2008, and the town is undoubtedly one of the most beautiful places I have ever been. While I was there, Stefano Sarti, the dairy's owner, and his family welcomed me into their home and showed me all that their farm had to offer—wild mint and lavender for the sheep to graze on, delicious honey, bright red tomatoes, and much more. I went there wanting to discover new cheeses and came away having learned some life lessons. Stefano contributes to his community in a truly significant way: all of his employees come from underprivileged backgrounds or have disabilities. They work together masterfully to make cheese, and we get to enjoy the fruits of their collaboration. I will never forget what Stefano and his team taught me, and I hope to one day make this recipe for the entire staff at Il Forteto Dairy.

To understand the different types of pecorino cheese,
see page 188.

CHEESE:
Queso Fresco

Marta Murga (of El Salvadoran descent) has been working at Cheese Boutique for just over 30 years. She's been an integral part of the evolution and success of the shop. When I was a child, she would bring these delicious, cheesy tortillas stuffed with tangy coleslaw. Marta always made me treats, and she taught me so much about cheese (she still does). I hope I do her justice in this recipe.

Tortillas à la Marta

PREP	25 minutes
COOK	16 minutes
SERVES	2

2 cups (500 ml) masa harina (corn flour)
1 cup (250 ml) lukewarm water
9 oz (255 g) queso fresco cheese, crumbled

1. Stir the masa harina and water together in a medium mixing bowl until smooth. Using your hands, knead the dough well until it is smooth. The dough will be quite wet when done. Cover the bowl with a towel, and let the dough rest for 10 minutes at room temperature.
2. Shape the dough into eight 2-inch (5 cm) balls. On a lightly floured surface, roll out each dough ball into 6-inch (15 cm) rounds.
3. Sprinkle the queso fresco cheese evenly over 4 of the rounds. Place a second tortilla over the cheese, and pinch the edges together to seal it. Leave a little bit of the tortilla open to allow steam to escape.
4. Heat a medium nonstick skillet over medium-high heat. Place the tortillas, 1 at a time, into the skillet, and cook for approximately 2 minutes on each side or until the cheese melts and the tortillas are lightly browned.
5. Transfer the tortillas to a serving plate, cut them in half, and serve with your favorite hot sauce.

Try coleslaw, refried beans, salsa verde, or anything that strikes your fancy with these tortillas.

Wookey and Waffles

PREP 15 minutes

COOK 25 minutes

SERVES 4–6

1¾ cups (440 ml) all-purpose flour

1 Tbsp (15 ml) sugar

2 tsp (10 ml) baking powder

1 tsp (5 ml) baking soda

1 tsp (5 ml) fine sea salt

3 large eggs, yolks and whites separated

1 cup (250 ml) melted unsalted butter

1 cup (250 ml) buttermilk

¾ cup (185 ml) soda water

Vegetable oil spray, for greasing

½ cup (125 ml) chopped thinly sliced country ham

⅓ cup (85 ml) grated Wookey Hole cheddar cheese

⅔ cup (165 ml) medium maple syrup (Go Canada Go!)

1. Preheat the oven to 300°F (150°C).
2. Heat the waffle iron over medium-high heat until it is very hot (I know you have a waffle iron somewhere; it's probably hiding behind your popcorn maker and fondue set, both of which I'm also going to make you use).
3. Whisk the flour, sugar, baking powder, baking soda, and salt in a large bowl. Set aside at room temperature.
4. Using an electric mixer, beat the egg whites in a medium bowl until medium-soft peaks form. Set aside at room temperature.
5. In a separate medium bowl, whisk the egg yolks, melted butter, buttermilk, and soda water to combine. Gradually whisk this mixture into the dry ingredients, then fold in the egg whites.
6. Coat the waffle iron with vegetable oil spray.
7. Pour enough batter into the iron to fill it, making sure to spread it into the corners. Scatter 1 tablespoon (15 ml) of ham and a scant tablespoon (10 ml) of Wookey Hole cheddar cheese over the batter. Cook for 5 to 7 minutes or until firm and golden brown. Transfer the waffles to a baking sheet, and place them in the oven to stay warm. Repeat with the remaining batter.
8. Serve with maple syrup.

CHEESE:
Wookey Hole Cheddar

I have yet to be in the Wookey caves, but my time is coming soon. Wookey Hole is a great cheddar, and while making this recipe, be sure to snack on this cheese while cooking. That's an order (and for a cool trick, try the cheese closest to the rind and then try the cheese farthest from the rind—do you taste a difference?). The next time you are at your favorite cheese shop, take a little tour of all the cheddars they have and see the differences between them all. And if you do this at Cheese Boutique, book the day off because you'll be tasting for a long time. I like to pair this cheese with a neutral flavor like waffles, because this cheese has to stand alone.

Relax Napolean,
It's Just Goat Cheese
Dumplings, page 80.

LUNCH

55   Niagara Summer Salad by Craig Harding

56   The Stella Salad

59   Big Shot East Coast Lobster Rolls

60   Bufala with Poached Pears and Toasted Pine Nuts by
       Claudio Aprile

63   Burrata Salad—Amazing to Eat, a Pain to Make

64   The Most Delicious Spanish Rice Ever

66   Fermented Ricotta Gnocchi by Rob Gentile

71   Hail Halloumi

72   Slam-Dunk Sandwich

75   My Ode to Stella Pristine Norwegian Corn Cakes

76   Peaches and Brie Grilled Cheese

78   Ragusano Soup by Jonathan Gushue

80   Relax Napoleon, It's Just Goat Cheese Dumplings

82   Rock and Roll Grilled Cheese

85   Tomato Pie by Chuck Hughes

86   Truffle Soup with Savory Comté Shortbread by Jason
       Bangerter

89   Very Much Alive Pasta

90   Warm Salad of Winter Radish by Anthony Walsh

92   The World's Best Frittata and I Can Prove It

95   You Will Make Friends with This Salad

CHEESE:
Ash Rind
Goat Cheese

Niagara Summer Salad
by Craig Harding

PREP	15 minutes
COOK	5 minutes
SERVES	2–4

4 medium-sized ripe peaches

7 oz (200 g) ash rind goat cheese

1 head cauliflower

2 Tbsp (30 ml) extra-virgin olive oil, plus extra for drizzling

Fine sea salt and freshly ground pepper

1 cup (250 ml) arugula

2 Tbsp (30 ml) good-quality aged balsamic vinegar (I like Balconville apple vinegar)

1. Preheat the barbecue to 350°F (180°C) or heat a cast iron pan over medium-high heat.
2. Using a sharp paring knife, evenly cut the peaches in segments around the pit on all 4 sides.
3. Cut the goat cheese into slices, about ¼ inch (6 mm) thick. Chop the cauliflower into small florets, removing the stem.
4. Take the sliced peach "cheeks" (as we call them) and toss them in a medium bowl with a splash of olive oil and some salt and pepper.
5. Place the cheeks, flesh side down, on the barbecue or in the cast iron pan. Allow the peach slices to cook for approximately 1 minute, then flip them over and cook for another 30 seconds. Remove the peach slices from the barbecue or cast iron pan. Remove the skin (it should slide off easily) and set the peach slices aside at room temperature.
6. In a large pot of heavily salted boiling water over high heat, blanch the cauliflower florets for approximately 45 seconds, then refresh them in an ice bath. Remove them from the ice bath after a few seconds, and let them dry on a clean dishtowel.
7. On a small side plate, arrange the grilled peaches, cauliflower florets, sliced goat cheese, and arugula. Just before serving, drizzle with extra-virgin olive oil and apple vinegar. Finish with salt and pepper to taste.

Everyone who follows me on social media knows about my special affection for Craig Harding, the chef at Campagnolo and La Palma in Toronto. Some of the best salads and pastas I've ever had were made by Craig. And to put the cherry on top, Craig is a great friend, too. One year on Boxing Day, when I had promised to host a Monopoly night for Craig, his wife Alex Hutchison, and my buddy Cory Vitiello, I had to put the kibosh on the whole thing when I realized I had screwed up an order for a client's wedding, and I needed to personally go to Cheese Boutique to fix it. Craig, Alex, and Cory pitched in with the prep, and we drove the order to Air Canada's cargo area to ship for next-day delivery to Newfoundland. Craig's recipe here is simple, but to get the most out of it, use the best ingredients you can find, exactly when they're in season.

The Stella Salad

PREP	1 episode of *Seinfeld* with commercials
COOK	15 minutes
SERVES	4

1 cup (250 ml) quinoa, rinsed and drained

7 oz (200 g) feta cheese, diced

2 medium vine-ripened tomatoes, diced

1 cup (250 ml) diced English cucumber (skin on)

⅓ cup (85 ml) finely chopped red onion

⅓ cup (85 ml) finely chopped fresh mint

⅓ cup (85 ml) finely chopped fresh oregano

⅓ cup (85 ml) extra-virgin olive oil

¼ cup (60 ml) red wine vinegar

1 clove garlic, minced

Sea salt and freshly ground pepper

Feta is such a nostalgic cheese for me. When I was a child, my parents painted the house, and the smell of the paint made me feel really sick. I was about 8 years old, and I had to stay with my grandparents for a week or so. Every morning, my grandmother, Stella, would make me chamomile tea and toast with feta—where our family comes from, feta is considered medicine. And I can't be certain, but I'm pretty sure that the feta made me feel better—at the very least, it was tasty. To this day, feta is my go-to breakfast or lunch cheese.

1. In a medium saucepan, bring 2 cups (500 ml) of lukewarm water and the quinoa to a boil, covered, over medium heat. Reduce the heat to low, leave covered, and cook for 12 to 15 minutes or until all the water has been absorbed. Remove the quinoa from the heat, uncover, and fluff using a fork. Set aside to cool, at room temperature, for 15 minutes.

2. In a large salad bowl, toss the cooled quinoa with the feta, tomatoes, cucumber, onion, and herbs.

3. In a separate bowl, whisk together the oil, vinegar, garlic, and salt and pepper to taste. Pour the dressing over the salad and toss well before serving.

CHEESE:
Smoked Provolone

Big Shot East Coast
Lobster Rolls

PREP	15 minutes
COOK	10 minutes
SERVES	4

A good friend of our family's, Derrick Luck, hails from PEI and inspired me to make this recipe. "Lucky" is one of our longest-standing customers; in fact, he's the third generation in his family to shop at Cheese Boutique. He happens to be a Denver Broncos fan, while I adore the Pittsburgh Steelers. Nobody's perfect, but this recipe is.

2 live lobsters (1½ lb/700 g each) or 4 frozen lobster tails (about 2 cups/500 ml cooked lobster meat)

1½ cups (375 ml) grated smoked provolone cheese

¼ cup (60 ml) 14% sour cream

¼ cup (60 ml) plain Greek-style yogurt

2 Tbsp (30 ml) chopped fresh dill

1 tsp (5 ml) lemon zest

2 tsp (10 ml) lemon juice

1–2 tsp (5–10 ml) sambal oelek (see note)

8–10 mini buns of your choice

1 medium avocado

8–10 small leaves spinach

1. Preheat the oven to 350°F (180°C).
2. To prepare the live lobsters, create an ice bath in a large pot or in the sink. Then, bring a large pot of 12 cups (3 L) of cold water to a boil over high heat. Drop the lobsters, head first, into the boiling water and cook for approximately 7 minutes per pound or until the shells turn bright red. Using tongs, carefully remove the lobsters from the water, and cool in the ice bath for 15 minutes.
3. If you use frozen lobster tails, allow them to thaw overnight in the refrigerator. Create an ice bath in a large pot or the sink. Bring a large pot of 12 cups (3 L) of cold water to a boil over high heat. Drop the lobster tails into the boiling water and cook for approximately 8 to 12 minutes or until the shells turn bright red. Using tongs, carefully remove the tails from the water, and cool in the ice bath for 15 minutes.
4. Using a sharp knife, crack the lobster shells and remove all the meat, discarding the shells. Coarsely chop the meat.
5. In a large bowl, combine the lobster meat, smoked provolone cheese, sour cream, yogurt, dill, lemon zest and juice, and sambal oelek. Mix well.
6. Heat the buns in the preheated oven for 3 to 4 minutes or until they are warmed through. Peel the avocado and slice it into thin strips. Divide the lobster filling among the buns, and top with spinach and avocado.

Sambal oelek is an awesome Indonesian chili sauce that can be found in many international grocery stores. If you can't find it, substitute harissa paste or a savory chili sauce.

Bufala with Poached Pears and Toasted Pine Nuts
by Claudio Aprile

CHEESE:
Mozzarella di Bufala

PREP 15 minutes, plus 4- to 24-hour resting time for rosemary oil

COOK 26 minutes

SERVES 2

POACHED PEARS

1 cup (250 ml) sugar
4 whole star anise pods
2 whole cinnamon sticks
10 whole cloves
4 medium Bartlett or Bosc pears, peeled

ROSEMARY OIL

1 cup (250 ml) olive oil
2 sprigs rosemary

1 loaf of country grain bread, sliced
1 cup (250 ml) honey
1 ball (7 oz/200 g) mozzarella di bufala cheese, torn into bite-sized pieces
Maldon salt
1 cup (250 ml) toasted pine nuts
Basil microgreens, for garnish

Claudio Aprile is one of the most avant-garde chefs and restaurateurs in Canadian history, and he is also one of my mentors. After having worked at El Bulli, listed as the number-one restaurant in the world for many years, Claudio came back to Toronto and revolutionized dining culture in the city with his focus on molecular gastronomy, precision plating, and simple ingredients. Over the years, Claudio taught me about Spanish cheeses such as Garrotxa, Montenebro, Zamorano, and others that have become best-selling staples at Cheese Boutique. And if that pedigree doesn't impress you, Claudio also happens to be a judge on one of my favorite food TV shows, *MasterChef Canada*. What a pro! Here, Claudio has shared his recipe for one of his most popular dishes—creamy mozzarella di bufala with poached pears.

1. To make the poached pears, in a large pot, combine the sugar, star anise, cinnamon sticks, cloves, 4 cups (1 L) lukewarm water, and pears. Poach, uncovered, for roughly 20 minutes over medium heat or until the pears are tender but still firm. Transfer the poached pears and their liquid to an airtight container, and set aside in the fridge until needed, or for up to 3 days.

2. To make the rosemary oil, in a small pot over medium heat, combine the oil and rosemary. Warm the mixture through, while stirring, for 3 to 5 minutes. Allow the rosemary oil to sit at room temperature, uncovered, for 4 to 24 hours. The longer it sits, the more intense the rosemary flavor will become. Strain, reserving the oil and discarding the rosemary.

3. Preheat the barbecue to 350°F (180°C).

4. To assemble, brush both sides of the bread with the rosemary oil, and grill for approximately 3 minutes on each side or until crispy.

5. While the bread grills, dissolve the honey in about 2 tablespoons (30 ml) of water in a small bowl. Stir well.
6. Thinly slice the poached pears.
7. Top the grilled bread with poached pear slices, mozzarella di bufala cheese, and a drizzle of rosemary oil. Season to taste with salt. Drizzle with the diluted honey, and sprinkle with pine nuts. Top with basil microgreens.

Burrata Salad—Amazing to Eat, a Pain to Make

PREP	3 minutes
COOK	N/A
SERVES	2

8 oz (225 g) burrata cheese (1 large ball, or 2 smaller balls)

8 medium-sized ripe field tomatoes, cut into wedges

12 small leaves basil, coarsely chopped

⅓ cup (85 ml) toasted Spanish Marcona almonds (can be found at a specialty food store)

1 cup (250 ml) baby arugula

¼ cup (60 ml) extra-virgin olive oil

Flaked sea salt and freshly ground pepper

8 thin slices Spanish serrano ham or Italian prosciutto

Aged balsamic vinegar, for drizzling

1. Drain the burrata cheese from its liquid and, over a large bowl, tear it into small pieces with your hands.
2. Arrange the tomato wedges and burrata cheese pieces on a serving platter. Top with basil leaves, almonds, and baby arugula. Drizzle with the extra-virgin olive oil, and season to taste with salt and pepper. Drape the ham around the salad. Drizzle with the aged balsamic vinegar.
3. The key to eating this dish is to get all the ingredients in 1 bite. *Buon appetito!*

When I was in Italy years ago, I visited a dairy that specialized in burrata (fresh mozzarella stuffed with fresh cream) and was invited to try my hand at making it. I thought it would be straightforward for a cheese genius like me (NOT), but I couldn't have been more wrong. There I was, on a cheese assembly line with about twenty 70-year-old women, and no matter how hard I tried, I couldn't line up the mozzarella cheese ball with the stracciatella cream nozzle. Either I made too large of a hole for the nozzle, or I injected too much cream and made the cheese ball break. Maybe I was just too clumsy for the task altogether. Any which way you put it, I failed, and all the Italian *nonnas* kept pointing at me and laughing. I never knew that little old Italian ladies could be so cruel (thanks for the heads-up, Mom). In this recipe, I won't ask you to try to make burrata, but I will say that getting the freshest summer ingredients is a must.

The Most Delicious
Spanish Rice **Ever**

PREP   15 minutes
COOK   35 minutes
SERVES 6

CHEESE:
Zamorano

Unsalted butter, for greasing

1 cup (250 ml) uncooked white rice

4 medium plum tomatoes, halved

½ medium white onion, finely chopped

1 clove garlic, peeled

¼ cup (60 ml) extra-virgin olive oil

1 medium serrano pepper, finely chopped

½ cup (125 ml) fresh shelled green peas (good-quality jarred
   peas will do too)

2 medium carrots, finely chopped

1 small Yukon potato, peeled and finely chopped

½ cup (125 ml) 14% sour cream

1 bunch fresh cilantro, finely chopped

Sea salt

5 oz (140 g) grated Zamorano cheese

1. Preheat the oven to 450°F (230°C).
2. Lightly grease a medium baking sheet with unsalted butter.
3. In a medium saucepan over high heat, bring 2 cups (500 ml) of
   water to a boil, and stir in the rice. Reduce the heat to medium,
   cover, and simmer for approximately 20 minutes, then remove
   from the heat. Do not stir.
4. While the rice is cooking, place the tomato halves, onion, and
   garlic in a single layer on the prepared baking sheet. Roast for
   10 to 15 minutes, flipping once, until the veggies are evenly
   browned. Remove from the heat, and let stand at room
   temperature until completely cool.
5. Purée the roasted vegetables in a blender or food processor.
6. Drain any remaining liquid from the rice.
7. Heat the olive oil in a medium skillet over medium heat. Add
   the serrano pepper, and cook for 4 to 5 minutes until tender.
   Add the rice, puréed vegetables, peas, carrots, potato, and
   sour cream. Season with cilantro and salt to taste. Cook for
   approximately 7 minutes, stirring, or until all the vegetables are
   tender and the rice is browned. Mix in the grated Zamorano
   cheese. Allow the cheese to melt before serving. *De nada.*

Zamorano is one of my
favorite Spanish cheeses. It's
made from sheep's milk and is
typically aged for 18 months.
Think manchego (see page 117)
but bolder, sharper, and much
better looking. I was introduced
to this cheese in Spain back in
2007. When I was in Barcelona,
I got tickets to an FC Barcelona
versus Real Madrid soccer
match. In the soccer world, this
is like Batman versus Superman,
Manning versus Brady, Godzilla
versus King Kong. It was an
epic match, with some of the
greatest players ever—David
Beckham, Fabio Cannavaro,
Lionel Messi, Thierry Henry,
and Ronaldinho, to name a few.
But as great as that game was,
I was almost more impressed
by the concession stand's
offerings: deep-fried pork rinds,
mini paella, and ham and
cheese on a crusty baguette.
And not just any ham and
cheese—this was acorn-fed
pata negra ham, and 18-month-
old Zamorano cheese. The
sandwich was so tasty that I ate
3 of them during the game.
The depth of flavor in the
cheese is equally amazing
with rice.

Fermented Ricotta Gnocchi
by Rob Gentile

PREP   1 hour, including the time to make the pasta

COOK   2–3 minutes

SERVES   2–4

1 batch ricotta and parmigiano gnocchi (see recipe across)

¼ cup (60 ml) high-quality unsalted butter

Pinch of sea salt

2 tsp (10 ml) lemon juice

1½ oz (40 g) grated aged provolone cheese

¾ oz (20 g) fresh, thinly sliced black truffle

1. In a large pot, bring approximately 5 quarts (5 l) of salted water to a boil. Sea salt works best here, and the water should have the salinity and taste of the ocean. As the water comes to a boil, heat a large saucepan over medium-high heat and assemble the butter, salt, and lemon juice for the brown butter sauce—you'll need to start the sauce as soon as you drop the gnocchi into the boiling water so that the pasta and the sauce are ready at the same time.

2. Cook the gnocchi over high heat for approximately 2 minutes or until they all float to the surface of the water. Remove the gnocchi from the pot and transfer right away into the sauce.

3. As the gnocchi cooks, brown the butter for 2 to 3 minutes. The butter should foam up and turn a golden caramel color.

4. When the butter has browned, add the gnocchi, and toss gently until the gnocchi are fully coated. Season with a pinch of salt and a splash of lemon juice. Taste to check the seasoning, and adjust if necessary.

5. With a spoon, plate the gnocchi and finish with the grated aged provolone cheese and truffle slices. Serve immediately.

I know him as "Handsome Rob," but all the foodies across North America know him as Rob Gentile, executive chef of the King Street Food Company. Rob is best known for his work at the Buca restaurants in Toronto. He's been a great friend for a long time. I made his wedding cake years ago by stacking beautiful Italian and Quebec cheeses to make a stunning and tasty cake. The 2 cultures represent Rob and his lovely wife Audrey's heritage. I remember how excited Rob was to tell me about Audrey when they first met, and in fact, one of their first dates was at Cheese Boutique. I showed them around, gave them a cheese tasting, and made sure to make Rob look good in front of his future wife. No matter how handsome Rob is, not many women can resist the charm of Cheese Boutique, right Rob? I've had some amazing meals at Buca, and Rob has regularly blown my mind with his mix of old Italian traditions and modern flair. This recipe might seem daunting, but I urge you to try it—you'll start blowing minds too!

CHEESES:

Aged Provolone, Parmigiano-Reggiano,

Ricotta di Bufala, Ricotta Salata

Ricotta and Parmigiano Gnocchi

MAKES   Just over 28 oz (800 g)

2 oz (60 g) finely grated Parmigiano-Reggiano cheese

9 oz (255 g) ricotta forte (see page 68) or high-quality cow's milk or sheep's milk ricotta

9 oz (255 g) finely grated ricotta salata cheese

2 large egg yolks

1⅓ cups (335 ml) all-purpose flour plus extra for dusting

1 tsp (5 ml) sea salt

1. In a large mixing bowl, combine the 3 cheeses, egg yolks, flour, and salt.

2. Mix well, using your hands, and then knead until the dough forms a ball. Be careful not to overmix. The dough should be just combined and smooth with the ingredients evenly dispersed.

3. Using a knife or pastry scraper, slice small, palm-sized pieces from the dough. Slice just enough to work with 2 hands. Cover the remaining dough with plastic wrap or a dishcloth to keep it from drying out while you work. Dust your work surface with flour, and roll the dough horizontally with both hands to create a tube shape ½ inch (1.2 cm) across (about the diameter of a nickel).

4. Cut the dough into ½-inch-long (1.2 cm) pieces. You can leave the pieces in a round, plump dumpling shape, or use different tools to shape them. At the restaurant, we roll pieces off a gnocchi board with our thumbs; you can use a fork or even the small holed end of a box grater, but be sure to dust the pieces with flour.

A NOTE FROM CHEF GENTILE: *Water content will play a big part in whether this dough comes together properly. At the restaurant, we use a very specific ricotta that we know works well with these measurements. You may have a really wet, fresh ricotta or a dryer, vacuum-packed ricotta. The fermenting process eliminates some water, so you may need to adjust the amount of flour in this recipe. Be open to experimenting and having fun. Your finished dough should not be sticky, nor should it be so dry that it is lumpy and not coming together. It should roll well without sticking to your hands.*

Ricotta Forte

MAKES   4½ lb (2 kg)

4½ lb (2 kg) ricotta di bufala cheese
1½ oz (40 g) sale di cervia, or another high-quality sea salt

1. Place the ricotta cheese in a large bowl and mix in the salt by hand until evenly incorporated. Set aside at room temperature.
2. Place the mixed ricotta into a sanitized fermenting crock or clay pot, and pack it down as much as possible. Place a layer of plastic wrap over the cheese, and make sure it's covered completely. Next, you need to weigh the cheese down. Some fermenting crocks come with round stone weights, or alternatively you can use a plate or even a resealable plastic bag filled with cold water to place on top of the ricotta. The plate or bag should be large enough to cover the ricotta completely so no air can come into contact with it. Cover your crock with a kitchen towel, and then place the lid on top. Leave the cheese to ferment at room temperature for 10 days.
3. Stir the cheese with sanitized spoons. Stir the cheese from top to bottom, very thoroughly, and pour out any excess water that has accumulated on top or under the cheese.
4. Pack the cheese back down into an even layer, and cover the same way you previously did.
5. Repeat this process every 10 days for 40 days, or until you have the flavor you are looking for. Once you have the flavor you like, refrigerate the cheese to slow fermentation. The cheese will keep for up to 100 days in a sealed container in the refrigerator.

Hail Halloumi

CHEESE:
Halloumi

Halloumi is slowly creeping into my Top 10 Cheeses of All Time (a list that's hard to crack). For me, this recipe is the ultimate summer lunch when the cheese and tomato are at their very best. In countries like Greece, Turkey, and Cyprus, halloumi cheese is part of the tradition, whereas in North America it's underrated and underused. But once you try it, you'll be hooked. I promise.

PREP	52 seconds
COOK	6 minutes
SERVES	2

1 package (7 oz/200 g) halloumi cheese
2 medium field tomatoes
Good-quality extra-virgin olive oil
Maldon sea salt
Freshly ground pepper
Good-quality French baguette

1. Preheat the oven to 350°F (180°C).
2. Allow the halloumi cheese to rest at room temperature for at least 20 minutes. Then cut it into 1-inch-thick (2.5 cm) strips.
3. Cut the tomatoes into wedges, and season them to taste with your good olive oil, salt, and pepper.
4. Cut the baguette into 1½-inch-thick (4 cm) slices. Place the slices on a baking tray, and bake for 2 to 3 minutes or until slightly toasted. Remove the bread from the oven.
5. Meanwhile, warm a medium pan over medium-high heat. Put the halloumi slices into the hot pan (you don't need oil or butter). Sear the cheese strips for approximately 3 minutes on each side, or until they are a deep golden brown. Be sure to serve the cheese hot; don't let it sit around!
6. Put the toasted bread on a large serving plate. Place the hot cheese overtop, followed by the tomatoes and an extra drizzle of olive oil. Enjoy the elegant simplicity of this dish. Enjoy the squeakiness. I told you this was easy.

This recipe relies on super-fresh and high-quality ingredients. Buy the best you can afford, and make this in the summer when the tomatoes are at their ripest.

Slam-Dunk Sandwich

PREP 15 minutes
COOK 17–19 minutes
SERVES 2–4

8 slices strip bacon

8 slices pumpernickel or rye bread

16 thin slices chili-gouda cheese

3 medium-sized ripe avocados

4 pitted dates, finely chopped

Fine sea salt and freshly ground pepper

4 Tbsp (60 ml) unsalted butter, divided

2 Tbsp (30 ml) extra-virgin olive oil, divided

1. In a small pan over medium-high heat, cook the bacon, flipping occasionally, for 5 to 7 minutes or until crispy. Remove from the heat, and place the cooked bacon on a plate lined with paper towel to drain excess fat.

2. Arrange 4 slices of bread on a work surface. Cover each slice of bread with 2 slices of chili-gouda cheese, but make sure not to let the cheese extend beyond the crust (or else). Divide the bacon evenly among the sandwiches. Peel and thinly slice the avocados. Add the avocado slices and chopped dates to each sandwich, and season to taste with salt and pepper. Top each sandwich with 2 more slices of cheese, and cover with the remaining bread. Press each sandwich down with the palm of your hand.

3. In a medium nonstick skillet over medium heat, warm up 2 tablespoons (30 ml) of the butter and 1 tablespoon (15 ml) of the oil. Place 2 sandwiches in the skillet, and cook for approximately 3 minutes or until the cheese melts. Flip, and cook the other side for approximately 3 minutes or until golden brown.

4. Transfer the sandwiches to a plate, and cook the other 2 sandwiches in the remaining butter and oil.

5. Cut the sandwiches in half before serving.

CHEESE:
Chili-Gouda

Spicy foods and me are like Shaquille O'Neal and Kobe Bryant: no matter how many championships we win, we just can't get along. But I do love spicy Dutch gouda cheese, so I've come up with a recipe that will make you think this LA Lakers rivalry never existed. Gouda is such an adaptable cheese and can be found in so many varieties: fenugreek, cumin, caraway, and cloves. For this recipe I'm going to use a chili-infused gouda. It has the perfect amount of heat and is a flavorful kind of hot as opposed to a take-off-the-paint kind of hot. This rich, flavorful sandwich pairs great with a beer or 2 (or 12, I'm not judging).

My grandmother, Stella, who helped Cheese Boutique flourish in the 70s and 80s alongside my father and grandfather, adored Jarlsberg. And she insisted that it had to be cut in square pieces, not wedges. This proved difficult, since the cheese comes in a large wheel, but my father and grandfather were both pros at doing it. As for me, though, I always struggled to cut the perfect square for her. I'm not sure why I couldn't get it, but we ended up with many 9-ounce (255 g) squares of Jarlsberg returned to the shop by my exacting grandmother. This recipe is dedicated to her, an absolutely wonderful lady. And don't worry, I didn't cut the cheese for this one.

My Ode to Stella Pristine
Norwegian Corn Cakes

PREP	15 minutes
COOK	20 minutes
SERVES	4

2 large eggs

2 cups (500 ml) fresh or frozen (thawed) corn kernels

¼ cup (60 ml) finely diced red bell pepper

2 Tbsp (30 ml) cornmeal

1 tsp (5 ml) sugar

¾ tsp (4 ml) sea salt

¼ tsp (1 ml) baking powder

4 Tbsp (60 ml) extra-virgin olive oil, divided

1½ cups (375 ml) grated Jarlsberg cheese

2 cups (500 ml) baby arugula

1. Preheat the oven to 350°F (180°C).
2. Separate the egg yolks from the whites in 2 small bowls.
3. In a large bowl, stir together the corn kernels, bell pepper, cornmeal, sugar, salt, baking powder, and egg yolks.
4. In a separate large bowl, using an electric mixer, beat the egg whites until stiff peaks form. Gently fold this into the cornmeal mixture.
5. In a large skillet, heat 2 tablespoons (30 ml) of the extra-virgin olive oil over medium heat.
6. Working in batches and using a ¼ cup to measure, drop the batter into the hot oil, flattening each corn cake slightly with a spatula, and cooking them for approximately 2 minutes per side or until golden brown. Transfer to a baking sheet, and repeat the process with the remaining oil and batter. If you notice the oil getting a little gnarly or too brown during the process, just toss it and replace with fresh oil.
7. Top the corn cakes evenly with Jarlsberg cheese, and bake for approximately 1 minute or until the cheese has just melted.
8. Remove from the oven, and make 4 stacks of 3 cakes each on the serving plates. Top the stacks evenly with arugula, and serve.

Peaches and Brie
Grilled Cheese

CHEESE:
Brie L'Extra

PREP	3 minutes
COOK	6 minutes
SERVES	1 hungry human or 2 regular humans

6 oz (170 g) ripe Brie L'Extra cheese

2 Tbsp (30 ml) peach preserves

4 slices hearty country grain bread, about ½ inch (1.2 cm) thick

3 oz (85 g) smoked turkey breast, thinly sliced

½ tsp (2 ml) chopped fresh thyme

1 Tbsp (15 ml) unsalted butter, divided

1. Cut the Brie L'Extra cheese into eight ¼-inch-thick (6 mm) slices, and set aside at room temperature.
2. Spread the peach preserves on 2 slices of the bread, just on a single side. Lay 2 slices of Brie L'Extra cheese over the preserves. Top the cheese with the turkey breast, and sprinkle with thyme. Place the remaining cheese slices on top, and close the sandwiches with the remaining slices of bread.
3. Heat a griddle or a heavy 12-inch (30 cm) skillet over medium-low heat.
4. Spread 1 side of the sandwiches with half of the butter, and place the sandwiches in the hot pan, butter side down. Spread the other side of the sandwiches with the remaining butter.
5. Cook for approximately 3 minutes or until golden brown. Flip the sandwiches, and cook, pressing lightly with a spatula, for another 2 to 3 minutes or until golden brown on the second side.
6. Slice each sandwich in half, and enjoy.

Brie L'Extra is a cheese I like to use as often as I can. It's super-tasty in this grilled cheese, paired with sweet peaches, but it works in so many other recipes as well. If you have ever used brie to make a pasta sauce, then you know how easy it is to use. Just place cubes of Brie L'Extra into a heated skillet and let it melt. Then toss your short noodle pasta in it, and season with freshly ground pepper. Booyah, that's not even the recipe for this cheese, it's a bonus one because I think you are a wonderful human being.

P.S. Leave Brie L'Extra out at room temperature for about 3 hours and enjoy with crusty baguette. It's such a tasty snack. Another added bonus!

Ragusano Soup
by Jonathan Gushue

CHEESE:
Ragusano

PREP	20 minutes
COOK	30 minutes
SERVES	6

1 small Vidalia onion, finely chopped

3 Tbsp (45 ml) extra-virgin olive oil, plus extra for garnish

Pinch of fine sea salt

1¼ cups (310 ml) 35% cream

1⅔ cups (400 ml) chicken or vegetable stock

9 oz (255 g) Ragusano cheese, grated

Freshly ground pepper

4 slices cooked crisp strip bacon, chopped (optional)

¾ cup (185 ml) green peas

1 bunch green onions, white and green parts, thinly sliced

Toasted breadcrumbs, for garnish

3½ oz (100 g) Ragusano cheese, shaved

1. Sauté the onion in the olive oil over low heat in a medium pot, with the salt, for approximately 3 minutes or until the onion is soft. Stir often so the onion does not color.

2. Meanwhile in a pot, combine the cream and stock, and bring the mixture to a simmer over medium-low heat. Remove the pot from the heat.

3. Stir the grated cheese into the onions until melted. Continue to stir slowly, and use a ladle to gradually add the warm cream mixture one ladleful at a time. When thoroughly incorporated, stop stirring, and allow the soup to simmer gently for approximately 5 minutes. Do not boil or the cheese will separate from the stock. Season with salt and pepper to taste.

4. Using an immersion blender, blend the soup in batches until very smooth.

5. To finish the soup, add the bacon (if using), peas, and green onions to the individual bowls. Divide the warm soup between the bowls, and garnish with extra-virgin olive oil, toasted breadcrumbs, and shaved Ragusano cheese. You can add freshly ground pepper to taste just before serving.

I first met Jonathan Gushue 15 years ago when he was the head chef of the famed Truffles restaurant in the Four Seasons Hotel Toronto. He went on to be the executive chef at Langdon Hall in Cambridge, Ontario, and is now the chef of the Fogo Island Inn. Jonathan has always been a dear friend and a much-loved presence at the shop: we've dined together, traveled together, and faced life's challenges together. He's my favorite Newfoundlander of all time.

If you store this soup in the refrigerator, you will need to blend it once more after rewarming. The vegetable garnishes can be adjusted for the season: try blanched fava beans, blanched chopped broccoli, or blanched sliced snap peas. In the summer, try sweet corn or cherry tomatoes.

Relax Napoleon, It's Just
Goat Cheese Dumplings

PREP   1 hour 10 minutes
COOK   25–30 minutes
SERVES   2–4

9 oz (255 g) Valençay cheese
¼ cup (60 ml) baby spinach
6 medium plum tomatoes
2 sprigs fresh thyme, divided
Pinch each of sea salt and freshly ground pepper
¼ cup (60 ml) crème fraiche
Zest from ½ fresh lemon
4 Tbsp (60 ml) unsalted butter
1¼ cups (310 ml) all-purpose flour
4 medium eggs

1. Place the Valençay cheese in the freezer for 1 hour. We are going to be grating this cheese, and since it can be quite soft, freezing it helps make it firm enough to grate. (I hope I don't offend anyone in France by asking you to do so.)
2. Turn on the oven's broiler.
3. Wash, drain, and shred the spinach. Set aside at room temperature.
4. In a medium pot, bring 8 cups (2 l) of cold water to a boil over high heat. Using a paring knife, gently score a small X on the bottom of each tomato—this will help you peel them. Using tongs, carefully place the tomatoes in the boiling water. After 2 minutes, remove the tomatoes from the water and peel the skin off them. Crush the tomatoes in a bowl using your hands (go Napoleon on them).
5. Place the crushed tomatoes and all their liquid in a large saucepan over medium-low heat. Add 1 sprig of thyme, salt, and pepper, and simmer for approximately 10 minutes. Then add the crème fraiche, spinach, and lemon zest. Give it a good stir, and reduce the heat to low. Simmer for another 10 minutes.
6. Take the frozen (I hope I don't lose my maître fromager title for doing this) Valençay cheese and grate half the pyramid onto a plate, rind and all.

Valençay is known for its unique shape, and there are many different explanations for how it got that way. The best one I've heard was that after Napoleon returned from a disastrous campaign in Egypt, he stopped in at the Valençay castle overnight. As he was sipping on a fresh Loire Valley white wine, a servant brought him a whole piece of Valençay goat cheese. Apparently, Napoleon was so furious with the sight of another pyramid that he took his sword and cut the top off the cheese, leaving it without its peak. This didn't make him feel better, but that's life. When you buy Valençay cheese, a good cheese shop shouldn't cut a pyramid of Valençay—it's a fresh creamy cheese so cut pieces won't hold up well, and honestly, let's not be as angry at cheese as Napoleon was.

7. In a large saucepan, combine the grated cheese, butter, and 1 cup (250 ml) of lukewarm water over medium-high heat. Bring the mixture to a boil, and season to taste with salt and pepper. Reduce the heat to low, and pour in the flour, stirring vigorously. Continue to stir until the dough forms into a compact ball.

8. Remove the dough from the heat, and add the eggs 1 at a time, stirring them in well. The dough should end up supple, not too hard and not too soft.

9. Using your hands, make dumplings approximately 1½ inches (4 cm) in diameter, just smaller than a golf ball.

10. Bring a medium pot with 8 cups (2 l) of salted water to a boil over high heat. Add the dumplings, and cook for 10 minutes or until firm.

11. Drain the dumplings, and place them in a single layer in a 9- x 13-inch (23 x 33 cm) oven-safe pan. Pour the tomato sauce overtop. Grate another quarter of the still-frozen Valençay cheese on top, and add the remaining sprig of thyme. Place the pan under the broiler for approximately 4 minutes or until golden brown.

12. Remove and discard the sprig of thyme and enjoy while warm.

Rock and Roll Grilled Cheese

PREP	2 minutes
COOK	6 minutes
SERVES	1

2 slices rye bread

4 tsp (20 ml) store-bought caramelized onion chutney

4 thin slices (3½ oz/100 g) Swiss emmental cheese

8–10 thin slices (3½ oz/100 g) beef brisket

4 tsp (20 ml) canola oil

Bread and butter pickles, for garnish

1. Heat a small skillet over medium heat.
2. Lay the rye bread slices on a clean work surface. Smother 1 slice of bread with caramelized onion chutney, and then place half of the cheese slices overtop. On the other slice of bread, place the remaining cheese slices, followed by the beef brisket. Carefully close the sandwich so that you have the brisket sitting between the slices of cheese.
3. Brush the canola oil on both sides of the bread, and carefully place the sandwich in the hot skillet.
4. Grill the beef and cheese sandwich on each side for approximately 3 minutes or until golden brown.
5. Cut the grilled cheese sandwich in half, and serve with pickles on the side.

CHEESE:
Swiss Emmental

When we moved from our old shop on Bloor Street in Toronto to our current location on Ripley Avenue, my dad organized a little parade. We had a vintage wheel of emmental cheese, weighing around 300 pounds (135 kg), that we were going to roll from the old location to the new location. It's not a long distance, maybe half a mile or so. We had very long red carpets, which we kept moving to keep the emmental from touching the ground. Looking back on it, it was an insane idea, but one of my father's best to date. With police officers leading the way, we had all of bustling Bloor Street staring at us. What started off with just my father, my brother, and me, with the 2 officers, ended with a few hundred people in a procession down one of the busiest streets in Toronto. We rolled that massive wheel of cheese to commemorate our big move after 30 years. I never looked at Swiss emmental cheese in the same way after that. It is now a special part of our family history.

Tomato Pie **by Chuck Hughes**

PREP	20 minutes
COOK	25–45 minutes
SERVES	4–6

7 sheets phyllo pastry or store-bought pie shell (deep-dish)
1 Tbsp (15 ml) extra-virgin olive oil, plus extra for garnish
¼ cup (60 ml) Dijon mustard
6½ oz (185 g) grated gruyère cheese
6½ oz (185 g) grated Canadian cheddar cheese
5 medium field tomatoes, in medium-thick slices
Fine sea salt and freshly ground pepper
Fresh torn basil, for garnish

1. Preheat the oven to 400°F (200°C) for a regular pie, or 350°F (180°C) for a deep-dish pie.
2. Stagger the phyllo sheets so that they cover the pie dish. Use a little bit of olive oil in between the sheets to seal them to one another. The phyllo dough should hang just slightly over the edge of the dish; trim any excess.
3. Brush the top of the phyllo with the mustard, and add the cheeses in an even layer. Place the sliced tomatoes on top, leaving room for the cheese to show through. Season to taste with salt and pepper.
4. Bake a regular pie for approximately 25 minutes, or a deep-dish pie for approximately 45 minutes or until the crust is golden brown.
5. Drizzle with olive oil, throw on some fresh basil, and serve.

Chuck Hughes is the chef and owner of some of Montreal's top restaurants, including Garde Manger and Le Bremner. He also has his own line of products such as olive oil, maple syrup, and pickled vegetables, which are available across Canada in top food stores. But most of all, he is a great friend of mine and a truly wonderful guy. When he did a tasting for his products at Cheese Boutique, he couldn't have been nicer to all our clients and staff. He's the real deal and a pretty badass hockey player to boot. Chuck recommends making this recipe in the late summer when the tomatoes are ripe and tasty. He also gives a huge shout-out to his Aunt Danie and his mom, who taught him this recipe.

Truffle Soup with Savory Comté Shortbread
by Jason Bangerter

CHEESE:
Comté

PREP	20–25 minutes
COOK	40 minutes
SERVES	2–4

6 sprigs fresh thyme

1 cup (250 ml) white onion, thinly sliced

6 cloves garlic, thinly sliced

½ cup (125 ml) sliced peeled celery

1 cup (250 ml) split, washed, and sliced leek (white part only)

¾ oz (20 g) fresh truffle (optional)

5 cups (1.25 l) sliced portobello mushrooms, about ¼ inch (6 mm) thick

1 cup (250 ml) Madeira

3–4 cups (750 ml–1 l) vegetable, mushroom, or chicken stock

3 Tbsp (45 ml) diced unsalted butter, cold

3 Tbsp (45 ml) good-quality truffle oil

Sea salt and freshly ground pepper

1. In a stock pot, sweat the thyme, onion, garlic, celery, and leek on low heat. At Jason's restaurant, they often have slivers, scraps, and end pieces of fresh truffle and use them in this soup (I say, la-di-da for Langdon!). If you don't have scraps of truffle lying around, but decided to buy some for this recipe, mince the truffle and add it here. Sweat until the vegetables are tender and delicious, about 10 minutes.

2. Add the portobello mushrooms, and cook for 3 to 4 minutes or until they soften and release their juices.

3. Reduce the liquid and deglaze with the Madeira. Reduce the Madeira until you have about ⅓ cup (85 ml) left in the pan.

4. Add stock until it just covers the solid contents of the pot and cook, covered, for about 15 minutes or until the stock has reduced by one-third and the broth is earthy and flavorful.

5. Take the pot off the heat and let it cool slightly. Remove the thyme stems.

6. Purée the soup using an immersion blender while still warm. When it is a smooth purée, add the butter, a little at a time, and follow with a slow drizzle of truffle oil to emulsify while you are still blending.

Jason "the Banger"
Bangerter is one of my very good friends and one of the most influential chefs in Canada. He oozes class and precision in all aspects of his life and his food. He trained with the great Anton Mosimann, one of the godfathers of European cuisine; worked with the Oliver & Bonacini Group for years when he led the kitchen at Auberge du Pommier; and has pushed Canadian food boundaries at the Relais & Chateaux property Langdon Hall in Cambridge, Ontario, for the last 6 years. If you want to have a dining experience to remember, go eat Jason's food—or better yet, try this recipe at home. He will make you think about what you are eating, and then he will make you swoon for more. Jason has always been at the top of his game and keeps getting better and more innovative. I love his food, and I love him even more.

7. Optionally, pass the soup through a fine-mesh strainer to make it extra silky, or you can choose to serve it as is. Taste and adjust the seasoning with salt, pepper, and a little more stock if needed. This soup works best served hot, but be careful not to boil it once you have added the oil and butter or the soup will separate. If you're making this ahead of time, reheat it over low heat and keep an eye on the temperature.

8. Serve with savory Comté shortbread (recipe below).

Savory Comté Shortbread

MAKES   12 cookies

¾ cup (185 ml) all-purpose flour
½ cup (125 ml) unsalted butter
½ cup (125 ml) finely grated Comté cheese
Pinch of fine sea salt and ground pepper

1. Preheat the oven to 350°F (180°C), and line a baking sheet with parchment paper.

2. In a bowl, mix the flour, butter, cheese, salt, and pepper with your fingers into a coarse crumb stage.

3. Using your hands, form the mixture into a dough, and let it rest, covered with a clean dishcloth, in a cool spot for 30 minutes.

4. Once the dough has rested, roll it out until it is ¼ inch (6 mm) thick, and cut rounds using a cookie cutter. Place the shortbread pieces on the prepared baking sheet.

5. Bake for 15 to 18 minutes or until golden. Cool before serving so the shortbread has time to firm up. These will keep in an airtight container at room temperature for a few weeks.

CHEESE:
Goat Cheese

Very Much Alive Pasta

PREP	15 minutes
COOK	18 minutes
SERVES	2–4

1 lb (450 g) rapini
⅓ cup (85 ml) extra-virgin olive oil
6 cloves garlic, crushed
1 tsp (5 ml) crushed red chili flakes
1 lb (450 g) dried orecchiette pasta
3 Tbsp (45 ml) grated lemon zest
Sea salt
6 oz (170 g) goat cheese, room temperature (see note)

I could have easily created 60 pasta recipes in this book, but I only have a few, so I need them to be special. Go to your local grocery store and get yourself the softest, creamiest goat cheese they have because this cheesy pasta recipe deserves it. It is a great meal for a nice springtime lunch with friends or family. I love this pasta dish because the goat cheese has a big presence, and as a no-sauce pasta, it is much lighter for the spring or summer heat.

1. Roughly chop the rapini.
2. Bring a large pot with 8 cups (2 l) of salted water (I suggest sea salt) to a boil over high heat. Prepare a large bowl of ice water. Add the rapini to the boiling water, and cook for approximately 4 minutes or until tender. Using a slotted spoon, transfer the rapini to the ice water. Chill, then drain the rapini. Pat them dry using a paper towel.
3. In a 12-inch (30 cm) skillet, heat the olive oil over medium heat. Add the garlic, and cook, stirring occasionally, for 3 minutes or until golden. Add the chili flakes, and cook, stirring constantly, for about 45 seconds to allow the flavors to infuse. Add the rapini, toss to combine the ingredients, and remove the pan from the heat.
4. Bring a medium pot of 6 cups (1.5 l) of salted water (again, sea salt is best) to a boil over high heat. Add the pasta, and cook for 1 minute less than the package's instructions specify.
5. Drain the pasta, and transfer it, along with the rapini, to the large skillet. Add the lemon zest, and turn the heat back on high. Toss to combine all the ingredients, cooking for about 1 minute, then season to taste with sea salt.
6. Divide the pasta between your serving bowls, and add a big spoonful of goat cheese to each.
7. Let the heat from the cooked pasta get the goat cheese rich and creamy, and enjoy.

The goat cheese to use here is the kind you can buy everywhere that comes in a vacuum-sealed tube.

Warm Salad of Winter Radish **by Anthony Walsh**

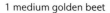

CHEESE:
Halloumi

PREP	15 minutes
COOK	45 minutes
SERVES	4

1 medium golden beet

1 medium sugar beet

7 oz (200 g) halloumi cheese, divided

1 large Valentine radish, sliced very thin on a mandoline

1 large Misato or green radish, sliced very thin on a mandoline

4 breakfast or Easter egg radishes, cut into quarters

1 cup (250 ml) sprouted lentils or peas

2 cups (500 ml) combined hearts of escarole, endive, and Treviso,
   torn into small bite-sized pieces

1 tsp (5 ml) thyme leaves

2 Tbsp (30 ml) flat-leaf parsley leaves

2 Tbsp (30 ml) lemon balm leaves (or 1 Tbsp/15 ml torn lemon
   verbena)

1 small handful of organic sprouts (whatever is fresh)

4 tsp (20 ml) good-quality maple syrup

4 lemon wedges

VINAIGRETTE

⅓ cup (85 ml) extra-virgin olive oil

¼ cup (60 ml) white wine vinegar

1 tsp (5 ml) Dijon mustard

Pinch of sea salt and freshly ground pepper

Anthony Walsh has been a mentor to me and a friend to my family for many years. In fact, at this point, he is family. He's shown up whenever we needed him, ready to pitch in and lend a hand, despite his insanely busy schedule overseeing thousands of staff and over 20 restaurants across Canada. He's a legend in the kitchen and holds a very special place in my heart. This recipe screams Canadiana and is a perfect reflection of one of this country's top chefs.

1. Preheat your oven to 375°F (190°C). Wrap each beet in aluminum foil, and poke a few holes through the foil with a fork. Roast in the preheated oven for 30 to 40 minutes, or until medium-soft. Once the beets have cooled enough to handle, dice them into bite-sized pieces.

2. While the beets are roasting, heat a small pan over medium heat. Cut off a ¼-cup-sized (60 ml) piece of the halloumi, and dice it into ¼-inch (6 mm) pieces. Place the pieces in the hot pan, and sear for 1 minute on each side. Remove the browned cheese from the pan and transfer to a small bowl.

3. In a large bowl, combine the beets, radishes, sprouted lentils, escarole, endive, Treviso, thyme, parsley, and lemon balm. Set aside at room temperature.

4. In a small bowl, combine all the vinaigrette ingredients. Stir well.

5. Dress the salad with the vinaigrette (reserve some dressing for the fried halloumi cheese, if you want).

6. Divide the salad between 4 serving plates, and grate the remaining halloumi cheese on top of each. You should use about 2 tablespoons (30 ml) per plate, enough to generously and evenly cover the salads.

7. Using a kitchen blowtorch, melt the grated cheese on the salads until it is just browned but not burned.

8. Top each salad with the fried halloumi cheese croutons and the sprouts. Drizzle 1 teaspoon (5 ml) of maple syrup over each salad, and serve with a lemon wedge.

The World's Best Frittata and I Can Prove It

PREP   20 minutes
COOK   40 minutes
SERVES   4

1 Tbsp (15 ml) unsalted butter, melted, plus extra for greasing

2 cups (500 ml) small broccoli florets

1 cup (250 ml) quartered mushrooms (halved if small)

¼ tsp (1 ml) fine sea salt, divided

¼ tsp (1 ml) ground pepper, divided

6 large eggs

¼ cup (60 ml) 2% milk

½ tsp (2 ml) dried thyme

1 cup (250 ml) shredded Glengarry Lankaaster cheese, divided

1. Preheat the oven to 425°F (220°C). Line a rimmed baking sheet with parchment paper.
2. Grease a 9-inch (23 cm) glass pie plate or oven-safe frying pan using unsalted butter.
3. In a medium bowl, combine the broccoli, mushrooms, melted butter, and half each of the salt and pepper. Spread the vegetables evenly on the prepared baking sheet.
4. Roast the vegetables for approximately 15 minutes or until browned. Remove the vegetables from the oven, and allow to cool slightly at room temperature.
5. Reduce the oven's temperature to 350°F (180°C).
6. In the same bowl or in a large measuring cup, whisk together the eggs, milk, thyme, and remaining salt and pepper. Whisk until frothy. Stir in half of the shredded Glengarry Lankaaster cheese.
7. Pour the egg mixture into the prepared baking dish. Sprinkle the broccoli and mushrooms evenly into the eggs. Bake for approximately 25 minutes or until evenly puffed and almost set.
8. Remove the dish from the oven, and sprinkle with the remaining cheese.
9. Turn on the oven's broiler, and broil for approximately 3 minutes or until the cheese is melted.
10. Serve immediately.

CHEESE:
Glengarry Lankaaster

My friend and colleague Margaret Peters is the owner and cheese maker at Glengarry Fine Cheese. In 2013, at the Global Cheese Awards in Somerset, England (the birthplace of cheddar), Glengarry Lankaaster cheese won the top prize for Best Cheese in the World. This is like winning the Stanley Cup, the World Series, or the Nobel Prize for cheese. And it couldn't have happened to a nicer person. Margaret is one of the humblest, most hardworking people I know. She didn't even want to enter her cheese in the competition because she didn't think it was good enough. I always called it Canada's finest, but I'm happy to be proved wrong, as it's now the world's finest.

"Bocconcini" is the fancy Italian way of saying "bite-sized." It's a super-fresh, mild, creamy mozzarella that comes in various sizes. I prefer—actually, adore—the cherry-sized bocconcini from International Cheese Company in Toronto, Ontario. The owner, Dominik, has known me since I was about 15 years old, and my entire staff at Cheese Boutique call him Uncle Dominik. I use a lot of his products because they are made with fresh ingredients and classic techniques. This kind of cheese is simple and straight-forward but works well in so many recipes, especially salads.

You Will Make Friends with This Salad

PREP	30 minutes
COOK	Nada
SERVES	4–6

2 cups (500 ml) baby arugula

1 cup (250 ml) grated carrots

1 large raw beet, peeled and sliced

¼ cup (60 ml) golden raisins

1½ Tbsp (25 ml) slivered or roughly chopped almonds

⅓ cup (85 ml) extra-virgin olive oil

¼ cup (60 ml) balsamic vinegar

Sea salt and freshly cracked pepper

2 medium red delicious apples, cored and diced

12½ oz (360 g) Santa Lucia cherry bocconcini cheese

1. Rinse the baby arugula under cold running water, then pat dry using a paper towel.
2. Place the arugula in a large bowl, and add the carrots, beets, raisins, and almonds. Gently mix.
3. In a small bowl, whisk together the oil and vinegar.
4. Pour the dressing over the salad, and season to taste with salt and pepper. Add the diced apple, and toss gently. Add the bocconcini (drop them right on top of the salad), and toss again to incorporate the cheese.
5. Serve while crisp and delicious.

Fondue à la Pristine, page 115

DINNER

99   Baked Pasta Quebecois-Style

100   Crispy Chicken Schwarzenegger-Style

103   Death by Pasta

104   Dungeness Crab, White Cheddar, Truffle,
         and Lime Mac 'n' Cheese by Ned Bell

105   Cauliflower Asiago Gratin by Michael and Anna Olson

107   The Dynamic Duo

108   Gattò di Patate by Modesta Pristine

110   Handmade Fusilli with Clams and Broccoli
         by Michele Forgione

112   Libretto Croque Pizza by Rocco Agostino

115   Fondue à la Pristine

117   Manchego Duero Paella Barbecue-Style

118   Melted Cheese and Pasta a.k.a. Mac and Cheese

121   The Monty Python Burger

122   My Mom's Meatloaf

125   No-Alarm Chili

126   Not So French Onion Soup (Part 1 of 2)

129   The Oaxaca Bake

130   Seafood Casserole by Rita DeMontis

132   Stuffed Cheese Pumpkin with Black Rice, Mushrooms,
         and Cheese by Daniel Boulud

134   This Quiche Doesn't Stink

Baked Pasta **Quebecois-Style**

CHEESE:
Oka

PREP 15 minutes
COOK 45 minutes
SERVES 2–4

---

1 small white onion, coarsely chopped
6 Tbsp (90 ml) extra-virgin olive oil
2 cloves garlic, minced
1 small eggplant, diced
2 small zucchini, diced
1 can (28 oz/796 ml) crushed San Marzano tomatoes
Pinch of fine sea salt and freshly ground pepper
12 oz (340 g) dried penne pasta
Fresh shredded basil, to taste
1 cup (250 ml) diced Oka cheese
2 cups (500 ml) grated Oka cheese

A few years ago, I was invited to visit Montreal, Quebec, to go on a tour of one of Canada's oldest cheese-making facilities, a Cistercian abbey that has been producing Oka cheese since 1893. In eastern Europe and some Scandinavian countries, it's traditional to eat an aromatic, nutty cheese like Oka at breakfast (god bless Europe). After 125 years, Oka is still hugely important to the Canadian dairy industry and is still a favorite cheese for many people at all times of the day. Let's all have a slice of good ol' Canadiana.

1. Preheat the oven to 350°F (180°C).
2. In a medium saucepan, sauté the onions in the olive oil over low heat for 2 to 3 minutes or until soft. Add the garlic and eggplant, and cook for another 5 minutes, stirring occasionally. Add the zucchini, and cook for about 3 minutes, again gently tossing. Add the tomatoes, salt, and pepper. Stir well. Increase the heat to medium, and continue to cook for approximately 10 minutes or until all the vegetables have softened.
3. In a large pot, bring 8 cups (2 l) of salted water to a boil over high heat. Cook the pasta for 1 minute less than the package's instructions advise or until al dente. Drain the pasta, and toss it into the sauce. Add the basil, and stir to combine all the ingredients.
4. Transfer the pasta and sauce to a baking dish large enough to hold it all. Add the diced Oka cheese, and stir well to combine. Sprinkle the top evenly with the grated Oka cheese.
5. Bake the pasta for approximately 25 minutes or until the cheese is melted and bubbly.
6. Serve immediately.

When you are buying this cheese, make sure you ask your local cheesemonger for a fresh young piece as there is nothing worse than an overripe Oka.

Crispy Chicken
Schwarzenegger-Style

PREP 20 minutes

COOK 15–20 minutes

SERVES 4

CHEESE:
Oka L'Artisan

4 boneless, skinless chicken breasts

1 Tbsp (15 ml) minced fresh ginger

1 Tbsp (15 ml) soy sauce

½ tsp (2 ml) sea salt, divided

½ tsp (2 ml) freshly ground pepper, divided

4 oz (120 g) Oka L'Artisan cheese, cut into 4 equal-sized sticks

¼ cup (60 ml) all-purpose flour

1 large egg

1 cup (250 ml) panko breadcrumbs

¾ cup (185 ml) grated Oka L'Artisan cheese

1 Tbsp (15 ml) honey, for serving

1 Tbsp (15 ml) grated lemon zest, for serving

In my baked pasta recipe (see page 99), I used the classic Oka cheese, but in this recipe, I'm using what is slowly becoming my new favorite, Oka L'Artisan. Once, a customer at the shop asked me what the difference was between the two, and I compared them to James Cameron's 2 *Terminator* movies. Both films are great in their own ways, and as technology evolves, so do both cheese and movie-making. After all, you can't make a great sequel without a classic to begin with.

1. Preheat the oven to 425°F (220°C) and line a baking sheet with parchment paper.
2. Slice the chicken breasts in half lengthwise, but not all the way through. They should open like a book.
3. In a large bowl, combine the ginger, soy sauce, and half of the salt and pepper. Add the chicken breasts, and using your hands, coat them well. Put a stick of cheese inside each chicken breast flap, and close well by patting it shut with your fingers.
4. In a shallow dish, combine the flour and the remaining salt and pepper.
5. In a second shallow dish, beat the egg with 2 teaspoons (10 ml) of lukewarm water.
6. In a third shallow dish, combine the panko breadcrumbs with the grated cheese.
7. Being careful to keep the cheese inside the chicken, coat the stuffed chicken breasts with the flour mixture, then dip them into the egg mixture, then roll them in the breadcrumb mixture. Make sure they are evenly coated. Place the chicken breasts on the prepared baking sheet.
8. Bake the chicken breasts for 15 to 20 minutes or until the chicken is cooked through.
9. Serve with a drizzle of honey and a sprinkle of lemon zest.
10. YOU'LL BE BACK for more.

Death by Pasta

PREP	15 minutes
COOK	15–20 minutes
SERVES	4

1 lb (450 g) dry linguine pasta (see note)
1 cup (250 ml) 35% whipping cream
1 tsp (5 ml) grated lemon zest
2 Tbsp (30 ml) unsalted butter
1½ cups (375 ml) sliced button mushrooms
⅓ cup (85 ml) chopped toasted walnuts
½ cup (125 ml) bocconcini cheese
4 oz (120 g) finely grated asiago cheese, divided
Sea salt and freshly ground pepper
2 Tbsp (30 ml) chopped fresh parsley

1. Prepare the pasta as per the package's directions.
2. In a small saucepan, stir together the whipping cream and lemon zest over medium heat. Simmer, uncovered, for approximately 15 minutes or until the cream has reduced by one-third.
3. Meanwhile in a large skillet, melt the butter, and sauté the mushrooms for 5 to 7 minutes over medium heat. Transfer the mushrooms to the cream sauce.
4. Drain the pasta, and add it to the cream sauce. Add the walnuts, bocconcini cheese, and half the grated asiago cheese. Stir well to combine. Add salt and pepper to taste, and sprinkle with parsley and the rest of the grated asiago cheese. Serve immediately.

Growing up with a southern Italian mother, I have pasta in my blood, but it's tough on the stomach. When I do make pasta, get ready for a cheesy, rich, I-wanna-take-a-nap-after extravaganza. Here, I want to take asiago cheese to the next level. Asiago originates in northern Italy, and is typically eaten as a "table cheese." If you're having lunch in the region of Vincenza, odds are that there is a piece of asiago the size of your head on the table. You're meant to pick at it over the course of a 3-hour lunch—in fact, Italians eat cheese as a digestive (god bless them). So, in addition to snacking on the asiago as I cook, my plan is to bring it up to super-cheesy-pasta levels.

When shopping for the pasta, try to find a bronze-die-extruded linguine. It's the good stuff! You can find it at most supermarkets and all specialty food stores.

Dungeness Crab, White Cheddar, Truffle, and Lime Mac 'n' Cheese **by Ned Bell**

PREP	20 minutes
COOK	35 minutes
SERVES	2–4

1 medium white onion, finely chopped

1 clove garlic, finely chopped

3 Tbsp (45 ml) canola oil

1 head cauliflower, stem removed and florets roughly chopped

8 cups (2 l) whole milk

½ cup (125 ml) 35% cream

1 cup (250 ml) mascarpone cheese

2 cups (500 ml) grated white cheddar cheese (I like clothbound Avonlea cheddar)

1 cup (250 ml) grated Grana Padano cheese

Zest and juice from 2 limes

2 Tbsp (30 ml) truffle paste

3 cups (750 ml) cooked and shelled Dungeness crab meat (you can substitute lobster meat or peeled shrimp)

2 Tbsp (30 ml) finely chopped chives

2 lb (900 g) pasta (your favorite kind), cooked

Ned Bell, Canada's sustainable fish and seafood authority, has taught me a lot about cooking and about fish and seafood in general—so much so that I credit him with my desire to one day open up a fish counter at Cheese Boutique. This recipe is rich and delicious, perfect for a cold night.

1. In a large pot, sauté the onions and garlic in the canola oil over medium heat for 4 minutes or until tender. Add the cauliflower and milk, and cook for about 20 minutes. Reduce the heat to low, add the cream and mascarpone cheese, and cook, stirring occasionally, for approximately 10 minutes. Be careful not to burn the mixture. Add the cheddar cheese and Grana Padano, and cook for an additional 4 to 6 minutes or until the cheeses have melted. Make sure not to let the mixture boil. Remove the sauce from the heat.

2. Using a slotted spoon, strain the cauliflower from the sauce, reserving the sauce. Place the cauliflower into a food processor and purée until smooth.

3. Transfer the puréed cauliflower back into the pot of sauce. Check the seasoning and adjust as necessary, and then add the lime zest and juice, truffle paste, crab meat, and chopped chives. Stir well. Add the cooked pasta, and stir until it's warmed through and coated well. Serve immediately.

This recipe is also great served as a baked pasta. Just preheat the oven to 375°F (190°C), transfer the pasta into a baking dish, and bake it, uncovered, for 10 to 12 minutes or until golden brown.

Cauliflower Asiago Gratin
by Michael and Anna Olson

PREP	15 minutes
COOK	30 minutes
SERVES	4–6

Two of the nicest people in the Canadian culinary community are Michael and Anna Olson. I first met Anna about 12 years ago when I was on her TV show talking about olives. Anna has written many incredible cookbooks, hosts multiple TV shows, and teaches. She's a pro in every way. Michael Olson is a great chef in the Niagara region of Ontario. He's a longstanding teacher at Niagara College, a sought-after consultant in many top dining destinations, and an author as well. I love when Anna and Michael come into the shop—they love my father's stories, and they sure love their cheese. Cauliflower and cheese are made to go together, but this version is a step up from the classic cauliflower with cheese sauce. It's easy enough to make for a weeknight supper, but dressy enough to go with your weekend roast.

Canola oil, for greasing
½ tsp (2 ml) sea salt
½ head cauliflower, cut into florets
2 cups (500 ml) 1% milk
2 Tbsp (30 ml) cornstarch
1 cup (250 ml) grated asiago cheese
¼ cup (60 ml) finely chopped sun-dried tomatoes
1 tsp (5 ml) finely chopped fresh oregano
1 green onion, white and green parts, finely chopped
Sea salt and freshly ground pepper
¼ cup (60 ml) dry breadcrumbs
¼ cup (60 ml) finely grated Parmigiano-Reggiano cheese

1. Preheat the oven to 400°F (200°C), and lightly grease a 6-cup (1.5 l) casserole dish with canola oil.

2. In a large frying pan, combine ¼ cup (60 ml) of lukewarm water and the sea salt over medium heat. Add the cauliflower florets, cover, and steam for 4 to 5 minutes or until tender. Remove from the heat, and set aside at room temperature.

3. Whisk the milk and cornstarch in a medium saucepan over medium heat until it has thickened and is just starting to bubble. Reduce the heat to medium-low, and add the asiago cheese, stirring until melted. Add the sun-dried tomatoes, oregano, green onion, and steamed cauliflower, stirring well to coat. Season to taste with salt and pepper.

4. Pour the cauliflower into the prepared dish. Stir together the breadcrumbs and Parmigiano-Reggiano cheese, and sprinkle the mixture over the cauliflower. Bake, uncovered, for 25 minutes or until the breadcrumbs have browned and the gratin is bubbling at the edges. Serve immediately.

The Dynamic Duo

PREP	10 minutes
COOK	22 minutes
SERVES	4–6 (or just my dog, Henry, who loves this dish as much as I do)

12 baby white or red potatoes
1 Tbsp (15 ml) salted butter
8 oz (225 g) cremini mushrooms, sliced
1 small white onion, finely chopped
6 slices Italian prosciutto, halved
9 oz (255 g) Swiss raclette cheese, grated

I consider raclette to be the Chicago Bulls of the 90s of melting cheeses (i.e., simply the best). Its properties scream for grilling or melting onto foods like toasted bread, pickles, apples, and cured meats. For me, though, the best food to pair with melted raclette cheese is a potato. For all you sport fans who love cheese, look at it this way: potatoes are to raclette what Scottie Pippen is to Michael Jordan. Whether they get along off the court or not, when it's game time, these two will shine. This recipe is perfect for a cold winter night when you're in the mood for a dish that will stick to your ribs.

1. Preheat the oven's broiler.
2. In a medium pot, bring 6 cups (1.5 l) of cold water to a boil over high heat. Add the potatoes, and cook for 10 to 13 minutes or until soft. Remove from the heat, and carefully drain the potatoes.
3. Transfer the potatoes into an oven-safe baking dish, and crush or smash them with a spatula (just like the Lakers got crushed by the Bulls in 1991, oh snap).
4. In a medium skillet, melt the butter over medium heat. Cook the mushrooms with the onion for about 6 minutes or until the liquid has evaporated and both the onions and mushrooms are starting to brown. Then, heat the prosciutto in the skillet for another minute.
5. Spread the mushroom mixture over the potatoes. Top with the raclette cheese, and melt under the broiler for approximately 3 minutes or until cheese is ooey and gooey. Serve immediately.

Gattò di Patate
by Modesta Pristine

CHEESES:
Ragusano, Mozzarella

PREP   30 minutes
COOK   40 minutes
SERVES 6–8 hungry southern Italians

3¼ lb (1.5 kg) Yukon Gold potatoes
⅔ cup (165 ml) warm 2% milk
4 oz (120 g) Ragusano cheese, grated
4 large eggs, whisked
Pinch each of sea salt and ground pepper
Pinch of ground nutmeg
3½ oz (100 g) salami cacciatore
5 oz (140 g) mozzarella cheese
2 oz (60 g) unsalted butter, plus extra for greasing
1 cup (250 ml) fine breadcrumbs

1. Preheat the oven to 350°F (180°C).
2. Wash the potatoes. Bring a medium pot with 6 cups (1.5 l) of water to a boil over medium-high heat. Boil the potatoes for 40 minutes or until they are tender. Remove them from the heat, and let them cool until comfortable to the touch.
3. Peel the skins off the potatoes, and place the potatoes in a bowl. Discard the skins. Add the milk, and mash the potatoes with a "schiacciapatate" (potato masher).
4. Transfer the mashed potatoes into a medium bowl. Add the grated Ragusano cheese, whisked eggs, salt, pepper, and nutmeg. Mix well using a wooden spoon. Set aside.
5. Cut the salami into small cubes, about 1 × 1 inch (2.5 × 2.5 cm). Then, cut the mozzarella cheese into cubes, about 1½ × 1½ inches (4 cm × 4 cm). Add both to the potato purée, and mix well using a wooden spoon.
6. Grease a 6- x 6-inch (15 x 15 cm) baking dish with unsalted butter, and then cover the bottom of the dish with the breadcrumbs, reserving a little bit for the top. Add the potato purée and spread it evenly across the dish, using a spatula. Sprinkle the top with the remaining breadcrumbs and little curls of butter.
7. Place the dish into the preheated oven, uncovered, and bake for 1 hour or until the top is golden brown.
8. Remove the dish from the oven, and let it stand for 15 minutes before serving. Serve while still warm. Buon appetito!

Modesta Pristine (my mom) is the most beautiful, talented, selfless, and caring person I know on this entire planet. A lot of who I am today and my love for food come from her, and I can't thank her enough for all that she does for me. This recipe is a real treat and reminds me of my youth. Some of the best times of my life have been sitting with my family eating gattò di patate. My mom's brother, my uncle Nicola, would usually come to Toronto once a year and stay for a good month with us. My whole family knew when he was coming to town because my mom would make her famous creation, as she knew very well that it was both my and my *zio's* favorite.

Il gattò di patate *is a classical Neapolitan recipe. The name comes from the French word "gateau," which the Neapolitan people changed into "gattò."*

Handmade Fusilli with Clams and Broccoli
by Michele Forgione

PREP 1 hour

COOK 20–25 minutes

SERVES 4–6

CHEESE: Parmigiano-Reggiano

1 cup (250 ml) boiling hot water

1¼ cups (310 ml) durum semolina flour (coarse), plus extra for dusting

Pinch of sea salt

¼ cup (60 ml) extra-virgin olive oil, plus extra for drizzling

4 Sicilian anchovies

3 medium garlic cloves, thinly sliced

2 tsp (10 ml) chili flakes

¼ cup (60 ml) dry white wine

1 lb (450 g) fresh clams

1 large head broccoli, cut into florets

½ cup (125 ml) freshly grated Parmigiano-Reggiano cheese (preferably aged 24 months)

1. In the bowl of a stand mixer with the dough hook attachment, combine the hot water and the flour. Add the salt, and mix for approximately 15 minutes or until the dough peels away from the sides easily. This dough can be kept in an airtight container in the fridge for 2 to 3 days, or frozen in a resealable plastic bag for 2 weeks. Just make sure to let the dough come to room temperature before using.

2. Cut the pasta dough in half and leave one half wrapped in a clean, moist dishcloth or plastic wrap so it doesn't dry out.

3. Take the other half of dough, and press it gently to create a flattened disc. Start working the dough through the pasta rollers, narrowing the distance between the rollers each time you pass the dough through until you've reached the halfway setting on the dial. You're looking to make a rectangle by the end of the process. Using a knife, cut thin strips, about 1 inch (2.5 cm) wide by 8 inches (20 cm) long. Toss them with a little bit of flour to keep them from sticking.

4. To shape the pasta, take 1 strip at a time and curl it around the end of a wooden spoon. This will create a spring-like shape. Repeat with the remaining dough. Gently place the finished pasta on a clean baking sheet sprinkled with a generous amount of flour.

Michele Forgione is the chef and owner of Impasto, Gema Pizzeria, and Chez Tousignant in Montreal, Quebec. I've been surrounded by food-savvy people and great chefs my entire life, but I've never met anyone who knows more about Italian food than Michele. I know it's a bold statement, but it's the truth. When I first met Michele, there was something about him that seemed familiar, but I couldn't quite place it. It turned out that he is from the same small Italian town as my mother! Avellino, just outside of Naples, is home to the best chestnuts, great white wine, and the Soprano family. And while this recipe might not be the "macaroni and gravy" that Paulie demands when the family goes to Italy, I think you'll love it even more. A pasta roller will help you make the pasta in this recipe; you can buy a roller that attaches directly to your stand mixer.

5. Fill a large pot three-quarters full of water and generously salt it. Bring to a boil over high heat.

6. Heat a high-sided sauté pan about 12 inches (30 cm) in diameter over medium heat. Add the olive oil and anchovies, and start breaking down the anchovies with a wooden spoon until they have melted in the pan. Add the garlic slices, and fry them until they are a light golden brown and fragrant, 3 to 5 minutes. Don't let the garlic brown too much, as you don't want it to become bitter. Add the chili flakes, and mix. Deglaze the pan with white wine, and let the wine reduce until the alcohol has evaporated and all that's left is a nice acidic note from the wine itself.

7. While the sauce reduces, clean the clams under cold running water until they start to release their sand.

8. Once the sauce is ready, add the cleaned clams, and cover with a tight-fitting lid. Steam the clams for 7 to 10 minutes to allow them to open, but do not overcook them. Remove any clams that have not opened.

9. Meanwhile at the halfway mark of the clams steaming, drop the pasta into the large pot of boiling salted water. Cook the pasta for 2 to 3 minutes or until it floats. Transfer the pasta to a large bowl as soon as it is done, using a slotted spoon. Keep the water boiling. Then add the broccoli to the pot of pasta water, and cook for approximately 5 minutes or until it is bright green but still has a bite to it.

10. Using a ladle or a measuring cup, reserve about 2 cups (500 ml) of pasta cooking water, and set aside until needed.

11. Add the pasta and broccoli to the sauce. Toss to make sure they are coated. If needed, add a little bit of the cooking water to the sauce to thin it out. Remove the pan from the heat, and add the Parmigiano-Reggiano cheese. Mix thoroughly.

12. Plate the pasta portions in nice deep bowls that have been warmed, then arrange the clams around the plate.

13. Sprinkle some additional Parmigiano-Reggiano cheese onto the pasta if you wish, and finish it off with a drizzle of the best olive oil you have.

I prefer the Planeta brand of extra-virgin olive oil from Sicily for this dish. You can make a tomato sauce version by adding either some tomato paste (triple concentrate) or a handful of ripe cherry tomatoes (wait until they burst and release their juices). You can also pop open a little can of Italian plum tomatoes—just a few will do. Add the tomatoes just before adding the wine. Tomatoes lend sweetness and acidity.

Libretto Croque Pizza
by Rocco Agostino

PREP	30 minutes
COOK	10 minutes
SERVES	2

10½ oz (300 g) dough ball (recipe across, or use store-bought)

"00" flour, for dusting

¼ cup (60 ml) béchamel sauce (recipe across)

¼ cup (60 ml) caramelized onions (recipe page 114)

3 slices cooked ham, torn into 1-inch (2.5 cm) pieces

½ cup (125 ml) grated gruyère cheese

1 Tbsp (15 ml) grated Parmigiano-Reggiano cheese

1 Tbsp (15 ml) olive oil

Flaked salt (optional)

1 Tbsp (15 ml) finely chopped chives

1. Preheat the oven to 500°F (260°C). If you have a pizza stone, place it in the oven to preheat as well.

2. Lightly flour the dough ball, and stretch it out to 12 inches (30 cm) in diameter. You can use your hands or a rolling pin, whichever you prefer.

3. If you are not using a pizza stone, place the dough on a well-floured baking sheet. Add the béchamel sauce on top of the dough and spread it evenly, leaving a 1-inch (2.5 cm) border. Evenly distribute the caramelized onions and ham overtop. Sprinkle the cheeses over the toppings and drizzle with the olive oil.

4. Slide the baking sheet into the oven (if using a pizza stone, slide the pizza onto the stone and place it in the oven). Bake the pizza for approximately 8 to 10 minutes or until the crust and the bottom are golden brown.

5. Remove the pizza from the oven. Season with salt if desired, and top with chives. Cut the pizza into slices, and enjoy!

Rocco Agostino, executive chef and part owner of Pizzeria Libretto, is the pizza king of Canada. I've known him for almost 20 years, and in addition to having a kind nature, Rocco is the authority on Neapolitan-style pizza. In fact, my parents prefer Rocco's pizza to any other kind in Toronto, as it reminds them of the homeland. For my father's birthday one year, we decided to order a ton of pizzas from Rocco—we stacked them all up, and the boxes were almost taller than me. Happy birthday to my dad, the real boss! (No disrespect, Bruce.)

Rocco Agostino's Pizza Dough

MAKES   Four 1 lb (450 g) dough balls—each ball makes two
12-inch (30 cm) pizzas or 10 individual pizzettes

1⅛ tsp (3.5 g) active dry yeast
1⅓ cups (335 ml) lukewarm water, divided
3¼ tsp (16 ml) kosher salt
18 oz or 3⅓ cups (500 g) "00" flour, divided

1. In a small mixing bowl, proof the yeast with 2 tablespoons
   (30 ml) of the water. Set aside at room temperature.
2. In the bowl of a stand mixer, combine the remaining water and
   salt. Add three-quarters of the flour to the water, and mix on
   low for 5 minutes.
3. With the mixer still going, add the yeast and the rest of the
   flour. Mix for another 5 minutes.
4. Stop the mixer, and let the dough stand for 10 minutes at room
   temperature. Restart the mixer, and mix for another 5 minutes.
5. Transfer the dough into a large container with a lid, and let
   stand for 14 hours in the fridge.
6. Portion the dough into balls, about 10½ ounces (300 g) each.
   Place the balls back in the container, covered, and let stand for
   5 hours in the fridge.
7. Use the dough balls right away, or you can place them in the
   fridge, in an airtight container, overnight to use the following
   day. Freeze any dough balls, in individual freezer bags, that you
   don't plan to use immediately. The dough will last in the
   freezer for up to 3 months.

Continued over

A NOTE FROM CHEF AGOSTINO: *I recommend making a large batch and freezing it in
balls. Defrost the dough for 3 to 4 hours before baking, making sure it's at room temperature
before prepping.*

Béchamel Sauce

½ cup (125 ml) unsalted butter
½ cup (125 ml) all-purpose flour
4 cups (1 l) half-and-half
1 Tbsp (15 ml) kosher salt

1. Melt the butter in a large pot over medium heat. Add the flour to the butter and mix well. Cook, stirring, for 2 minutes. You don't want the mixture to get any color. Add the half-and-half and salt, and whisk the mixture constantly, making sure to get any flour stuck in the corners and on the sides of the pot.
2. Once the mixture thickens to a yogurt-like consistency, remove it from the heat and strain it through a mesh strainer into a large container. Cool the sauce completely at room temperature, then place it in the fridge, covered, or use it immediately. The sauce will keep for up to 1 week.

Caramelized Onions

5 medium cooking onions, thinly sliced
¼ cup (60 ml) unsalted butter
4 stems rosemary
¼ cup (60 ml) honey

1. Place the onions, butter, rosemary, and honey in a large pot over medium heat. Mix well. Cook, uncovered, for 30 minutes or until the mixture starts to caramelize and the onions start turning golden brown. Stir occasionally to prevent the onions from sticking to the pot.
2. Transfer the mixture to an airtight container and cool completely at room temperature. Cover, and keep in the fridge until needed or for up to 1 week.

Switzerland was the first
European country that I visited
to learn to make cheese. So
how could I possibly write a
cheese cookbook and not
include a recipe for fondue,
which is the unofficial national
dish of Switzerland? That just
wouldn't be right.

Fondue **à la Pristine**

PREP	15 minutes
COOK	12 minutes
SERVES	2–4

2 cups (500 ml) grated emmental cheese

2 cups (500 ml) grated gruyère cheese

1 Tbsp (15 ml) cornstarch

1 cup (250 ml) your favorite lager

1 large clove garlic, halved and lightly smashed

1 Tbsp (15 ml) finely chopped thyme

¼ cup (60 ml) Kirsch or Grand Marnier liqueur

Freshly ground pepper

GARNISHES FOR DIPPING

1 large honeycrisp or royal gala apple, cored and cut into wedges

8 boiled new potatoes (or another vegetable if you wish)

Crusty baguette, cubed

Landjaeger sausage, sliced (see note)

Another hard-cured sausage (chorizo or whatever you like), sliced

1 large raw red bell pepper, coarsely chopped

1. In a large bowl, toss the cheeses with the cornstarch.
2. In a 3-quart (3 l) saucepan, combine the beer and garlic. Bring the mixture almost to a boil, uncovered over medium-high heat. Turn off the heat, and allow the mixture to rest for approximately 5 minutes. Remove and discard the garlic.
3. Return the pan to the stove over medium-low heat. Add the cheese mixture a large handful at a time, stirring each batch so that the cheese doesn't clump as it melts. This is a crucial point in the method: keep your eye on it and stir constantly but slowly. Continue until all the cheese is melted and the mixture is smooth and thick. Adjust the heat if necessary to maintain a simmer. Stir the thyme and liqueur into the cheese mixture, and season to taste with pepper. When the flavors have combined, and the cheese is melted, it is ready to serve.
4. To serve, transfer the mixture to a fondue pot. Set the fondue over a low flame to keep it warm. Serve with all your beautiful garnish items and enjoy a nice cold beer (or 2) with it.

The landjaeger sausage, which is a Swiss-German hard beef sausage, can be hard to find, but high-end European delis will likely have it. Try there first!

Manchego cheese is one of Spain's most prized ingredients. I think it's one of the top 10 cheeses ever created, and it works so well in this recipe. It also goes well with a glass of rioja red wine. In fact, manchego duero and rioja are like Spain's version of peanut butter and jelly—a perfect marriage.

Manchego Duero Paella
Barbecue-Style

PREP	20 minutes
COOK	30 minutes
SERVES	4–6

1 Tbsp (15 ml) salted butter

2 skinless, boneless chicken breasts, cubed

1 medium white onion, finely chopped

2 cloves garlic, finely chopped

½ cup (125 ml) tomato sauce

1 tsp (5 ml) ground Espelette pepper

1 tsp (5 ml) smoked paprika

2 pinches each of sea salt and ground pepper

1 cup (250 ml) uncooked paella rice (*arroz bomba*)

5 oz (140 g) uncooked shrimp, shelled and rinsed

2 medium zucchini, quartered lengthwise

6 oz (170 g) coarsely shredded manchego duero cheese (aged 3 months)

1. Preheat the barbecue to 475°F (240°C).
2. Preheat a large cast iron skillet (my favorite type is Le Creuset) or an aluminum pie plate on the barbecue for 2 to 3 minutes with the lid open.
3. Melt the butter in the hot skillet or in the pie plate, and brown the chicken along with the onion and garlic, stirring, for 3 to 5 minutes. Add the tomato sauce, ground Espelette pepper, paprika, salt, and pepper. Bring the mixture to a boil.
4. Once the tomato sauce is boiling, add the rice and 1½ cups (375 ml) lukewarm water, and cover tightly with aluminum foil. Cook the rice, with the barbecue lid up, for approximately 10 minutes. Then carefully add the shrimp, cover with the aluminum foil again, and continue to cook, barbecue lid down, for an additional 10 minutes or until the rice is tender. Remove the skillet from the grill and set aside.
5. Place the zucchini quarters directly on the grill, with the lid open, and cook them for 4 minutes, flipping halfway through the cooking time, or until grill marks appear. Remove the zucchini from the grill, and cut it into even-sized strips.
6. Top the paella with zucchini strips and manchego duero cheese. Serve immediately.

Melted Cheese and Pasta
a.k.a. Mac and Cheese

PREP	15 minutes
COOK	60 minutes
SERVES	12

1 lb (450 g) fresh plum tomatoes

6 cups (1.5 l) broccoli florets

2 Tbsp (30 ml) extra-virgin olive oil

1 lb (450 g) dried penne pasta

3 Tbsp (45 ml) unsalted butter

3 Tbsp (45 ml) all-purpose flour

4 cups (1 l) 2% milk

2⅓ cups (575 ml) grated aged asiago cheese

2½ cups (625 ml) grated aged cheddar cheese

1½ tsp (7 ml) fine sea salt

2 tsp (10 ml) freshly ground pepper

2 Tbsp (30 ml) chopped fresh thyme

1. Preheat the oven to 400°F (200°C) and line a baking sheet with parchment paper.
2. Cut the tomatoes into ¼-inch-thick (6 mm) slices.
3. In a large bowl, toss the tomatoes and broccoli with the olive oil. Transfer them to the prepared baking sheet, and roast for 30 minutes.
4. Meanwhile, in a medium pot, bring 8 cups (2 l) of salted water to a boil over high heat. Cook the pasta, stirring occasionally, for 8 to 10 minutes or until al dente. Remove the pasta from the heat, drain, and set aside in the pot until needed.
5. Whisk together the butter and flour in large pot over medium-high heat for 2 minutes or until it forms a thick paste (a roux). Add the milk, and whisk vigorously for 3 minutes or until the mixture thickens and bubbles. Remove from the heat.
6. Whisk the cheeses, salt, pepper, and thyme into the pot. Stir in the cooked pasta and roasted broccoli, and transfer into a 9- × 13-inch (23 × 33 cm) baking dish. Top with the roasted tomatoes, and bake for 30 minutes or until golden brown on top.
7. Serve immediately.

I was planning to write this cookbook without a macaroni and cheese recipe, but everyone said that was crazy talk. Fine, you guys win. There is no right or wrong answer as to what cheese you should put into your mac and cheese. Pick any other 2 cheeses in this cookbook and try out this recipe. Trust me, you can never really go wrong with melted cheese and pasta. Gruyère, cheddar, fontina, mozzarella, gouda, havarti (gross, by the way; see page 158), asiago, muenster, edam, and Monterey Jack—they will all work, and in any combination, too. When you go shopping for your cheese, try a few of these and see what flavors you prefer, but don't buy any pre-sliced or pre-grated cheeses, please. My hope is that you have fun with this recipe. Let the dish remind you of your youth. Some last food for thought: I've judged many mac and cheese competitions, and the winners were always the simplest, tastiest, and creamiest.

The **Monty Python** Burger

CHEESE:

Abbot's Gold Caramelised Onion Cheddar

PREP	20 minutes
COOK	10 minutes
SERVES	4

1 lb (450 g) ground sirloin beef

1 lb (450 g) ground lamb

1 clove garlic, crushed

1 small white onion, grated

1 tsp (5 ml) dried oregano

1 Tbsp (15 ml) dried parsley

Sea salt and freshly ground pepper

8 slices Abbot's Gold Caramelised Onion Cheddar, cut ¼ inch (6 mm) thick

4 good-quality burger buns

Your favorite burger toppings (see note)

Caramelized onions are a traditional condiment for burgers in the United Kingdom and North America. So my thinking was to take a burger patty's 2 best friends (caramelized onions and cheddar cheese) and put them together to make 1 magical burger ingredient. It's so easy, and you will look like the burger master in front of all your friends. Once the heat hits that cheese, look out for the incredible aroma that will come out of your barbecue.

1. Preheat the barbecue to 350°F (180°C).

2. In a large bowl, combine the beef, lamb, garlic, onion, oregano, and parsley. With wet (and preferably clean) hands, mix the ingredients together and form the meat into 1½-inch-thick (4 cm) patties, made to fit the size of the wicked burger buns you promised you would buy.

3. On a clean work surface, press each patty in the middle with your finger to create a dimple. This will allow the burger to keep its shape and will even out the cooking temperature. Sprinkle the burger patties with salt and pepper.

4. Grill the burger patties, flipping only once, for approximately 5 minutes per side or until the internal temperature reaches 160°F (70°C) (for those of you with a fancy meat thermometer). About 2 minutes before the burgers are done, top them with cheese.

5. Let the burgers rest for 1 minute off the heat, allowing the cheese to continue melting, and then place the burgers on the buns and dress appropriately.

If you don't like lamb (well, no one is perfect), just use beef. I won't tell you how to dress your burgers, but in this recipe, the cheese has a lot going already, so try to keep it minimal. If I were you, a good sliced pickle and a touch of barbecue sauce would make me a happy camper.

My Mom's Meatloaf

PREP	20 minutes
COOK	55 minutes
SERVES	4–6 hungry teenage boys

CHEESE:
Feta

¾ cup (185 ml) whole wheat couscous

1 tsp (5 ml) dried oregano

1 tsp (5 ml) ground cumin

½ tsp (2 ml) ground pepper

½ tsp (2 ml) sea salt

½ cup (125 ml) 2% milk

1 large egg

1½ lb (700 g) lean ground beef

½ cup (125 ml) crumbled feta cheese (Greek or Bulgarian feta is ideal)

TOPPING

1½ cups (375 ml) coarsely chopped plum tomatoes

½ tsp (2 ml) dried oregano

¼ tsp (1 ml) ground pepper

½ cup (125 ml) crumbled feta cheese

1 tsp (5 ml) grated lemon zest

1 Tbsp (15 ml) freshly squeezed lemon juice

1. Preheat the oven to 350°F (180°C).

2. Line a 9- × 5-inch (23 × 13 cm) metal loaf pan with aluminum foil. Using the tip of a knife, poke a small hole in each of the bottom corners of the foil to help the cooking liquid drain out.

3. In a large bowl, combine the couscous, oregano, cumin, pepper, sea salt, and milk. Allow the mixture to soak, uncovered, for approximately 15 minutes at room temperature.

4. Add the egg to the couscous mixture, and using a fork, mix it all together until well blended. Add the ground beef and feta cheese, and mix gently to combine.

5. Press the meat mixture into the prepared loaf pan. Flatten the top so it's smooth, and bake for 40 minutes. To test for doneness, poke a small hole in the middle of the meatloaf with a toothpick. If the juices run clear, you're done.

6. While the meatloaf is cooking, prepare the topping. Place the tomatoes in a strainer, and set them over a bowl to drain off the excess liquid.

When I was growing up, my mom never cooked traditional North American meals. We didn't have things like hot dogs, casseroles, or even roasts. When my friends came over, my mom, who is the most hospitable person I've ever met, always tried to feed us. After a long game of street hockey, all my friends wanted to eat were burgers and fries, but instead my mom gave us all stuffed bell peppers with rice and ground beef served with goat's milk yogurt. Yuck. No one liked it but me. But this is Mediterranean cuisine: it's what I was used to, and I thought this was all there was to eat. This recipe is my version of a dish created by my lovely mother. One day she finally caved and made something all my friends would recognize, but at least she made it her own.

7. In a medium bowl, combine the oregano, pepper, feta cheese, lemon zest, and lemon juice. Allow this mixture to marinate at room temperature while the meatloaf is baking.

8. Stir the drained tomatoes into the marinated feta mixture. Either discard the tomato liquid or make the best Caesar of all time with it.

9. Remove the meatloaf from the oven, and spoon the tomato mixture evenly on top, pressing lightly. Bake the meatloaf for an additional 15 minutes, no more and no less—it will be cooked perfectly.

10. Remove the meatloaf from the oven and allow it to rest for 10 minutes. Carefully lift the aluminum foil to remove the meatloaf from the pan, and let the excess liquid drain off through the holes.

11. Slice and serve immediately. This dish is not to be eaten with ketchup . . . or you will have to answer to Mrs. Modesta Pristine.

I'm not a huge fan of heat, so I would rather my chili be cheesy than spicy. This recipe has tons of flavor without the traditional fieriness of your everyday chili.

No-Alarm Chili

PREP	10 minutes
COOK	20 minutes
SERVES	4

1 Tbsp (15 ml) extra-virgin olive oil
1 medium white onion, diced
2 cloves garlic
1 lb (454 g) lean ground beef
4 cups (1 l) chicken stock
1 can (14 oz/398 ml) diced tomatoes
¾ cup (185 ml) canned white kidney beans, drained and rinsed
¾ cup (185 ml) canned red kidney beans, drained and rinsed
2 tsp (10 ml) chili powder
1½ tsp (7 ml) ground cumin
Fine sea salt and ground pepper
5 oz (140 g) dried tubetti (or another short noodle pasta)
1 cup (250 ml) shredded Red Fox cheese
Small handful of freshly chopped flat-leaf parsley

1. Heat the olive oil in a large skillet or Dutch oven over medium-high heat. Sweat the onions for 2 minutes, and then add the garlic and ground beef. Cook, stirring occasionally, for 3 to 5 minutes or until the beef has browned. Make sure to crumble the beef as it cooks, and then drain the excess fat with a spoon if needed.

2. Stir in the chicken stock, tomatoes, beans, chili powder, and cumin. Season to taste with salt and pepper. Bring the mixture to a simmer and stir in the pasta. Cover with a tight-fitting lid, and bring the chili to a boil. Then reduce the heat to low, and simmer for 13 to 15 minutes or until cooked.

3. Remove the skillet from the heat. Top the chili with cheese, and cover for approximately 2 minutes or until the cheese has completely melted. Garnish with parsley, and serve immediately.

Not So French Onion Soup (Part 1 of 2)

PREP	15 minutes
COOK	1 hour 15 minutes
SERVES	4

3 Tbsp (45 ml) olive oil

5 medium Vidalia onions, thinly sliced

A couple of pinches of sea salt

1 tsp (5 ml) sugar

1 cup (250 ml) dry white wine

4 sprigs fresh thyme

1 tsp (5 ml) dried marjoram (or another aromatic dried herb)

6 cups (1.5 l) beef stock

Sea salt and freshly ground pepper

1 loaf of good-quality crusty bread

2 cups (500 ml) grated Auricchio Provolone cheese

1. Preheat the oven to 350°F (180°C).
2. Place the olive oil in a heavy-bottomed pot over medium heat. Once the oil is shimmering, add the onions, 1 tablespoon (15 ml) of lukewarm water, and the salt. Cook the onions for 15 minutes, stirring, or until soft. Then add the sugar, and reduce the heat to low. Continue to stir the onions often, and cook for an additional 20 minutes or until they are light golden brown, have shrunk significantly, and are caramelized.
3. Once the onions have caramelized, raise the heat back to medium. Add the white wine, thyme, and marjoram. Allow the wine to reduce by half, stirring occasionally. Stir in the beef stock, and season with salt and pepper to taste. Simmer for 30 to 40 minutes.
4. Cut the bread into 1-inch (2.5 cm) cubes. Place the cubes on a baking tray and toast in the preheated oven, flipping them halfway through the cooking time, for 5 to 7 minutes, or until golden brown and toasted.
5. Turn on the oven's broiler.
6. Ladle the soup into 4 ovenproof soup bowls. Place a toasted piece of bread in each bowl, and divide the grated Auricchio Provolone cheese evenly between the bowls. Place the soup bowls on a pizza tray or thin baking sheet, and broil them for 3 to 4 minutes or until the cheese is bubbly and slightly browned.
7. Place the bowls on dinner napkins and then on a plate to serve.

CHEESE:
Auricchio Provolone

At Cheese Boutique, we get about 20 deliveries a day from our suppliers, with about 15,000 ingredients from all over the world: everything from cheese to saffron to sides of cattle—I've almost seen it all. Our loading dock can be a chaotic place with so much hustle and bustle from the minute we open to the minute we close. One day in September 2009, a monster of a delivery arrived at the shop: a 900-pound (400 kg) Auricchio Provolone cheese from northern Italy, a torpedo-shaped behemoth standing over 10 feet (3 m) high. Those of us on the loading dock gasped at the sight of it. It was like the supplier had dropped off a stegosaurus. This cheese was massive. We had planned to hang it in our cheese aging room, but that was easier said than done. It took days to figure out how to maneuver it through the shop and into the cheese cave. Carts, trolleys, a pulley system, brute force—we tried everything. Finally, we got this huge cheese into the cheese cave, and we did eventually hang it in the traditional manner, although we had to reinforce the ceiling to handle the weight. What an ordeal it was, but one does crazy things for love (of cheese). To this day, the Auricchio Provolone cheese hangs proudly in our aging room. I probe it (relax, it's a cheese term) for quality every few months. It's nowhere near ready to be cut down, but when it is, look out: it will be an umami explosion. So, the moral to this recipe is, when shopping for this cheese, try to find the oldest possible. The more aged this cheese is, the more developed in flavor and the better your dish will be.

The **Oaxaca** Bake

PREP	10 minutes
COOK	35 minutes
SERVES	4

Around 2007, Toronto was taken over by a taco craze. You saw them on every restaurant menu, and it seemed that a new "best taco" list was coming out every week. There was no escaping it. When I think of this time, I always come back to Oaxaca cheese (pronounced "wa-HA-ca"), which is perfect for tacos. But that's not all it's good for. After all this taco talk, I'm going to throw you a nasty curveball. I'm going to be blasphemous and use Oaxaca cheese in a non-taco dish (you know me; I have to be different).

Unsalted butter, for greasing
1 can (19 oz/540 ml) black beans or kidney beans, drained and rinsed
1 cup (250 ml) corn kernels, thawed if frozen
¾ cup (185 ml) chunky mild salsa (use medium or hot if you would prefer)
2 Tbsp (30 ml) chopped fresh cilantro
2 tsp (10 ml) chili powder
½ tsp (2 ml) ground cumin
4 small whole wheat tortillas, each about 7 inches (18 cm) in diameter
1¼ cups (310 ml) halved cherry or grape tomatoes, divided
1 cup (250 ml) shredded Oaxaca cheese, divided
¼ cup (60 ml) broken tortilla chips
4 kalamata olives, pitted and halved

1. Preheat the oven to 350°F (180°C).
2. Grease a 7- × 11-inch (18 × 28 cm) baking dish with the butter.
3. In a medium bowl, coarsely mash the beans. Stir in the corn, salsa, cilantro, chili powder, and cumin.
4. Place 2 tortillas overlapping across the bottom of the prepared baking dish. Spread half of the bean mixture over the tortillas. Top with ½ cup (125 ml) of tomatoes and sprinkle with ⅓ cup (85 ml) of Oaxaca cheese. Top with the remaining tortillas, followed by the rest of the bean mixture, then ½ cup (125 ml) of tomatoes, and ⅓ cup (85 ml) of cheese.
5. Bake for approximately 25 minutes or until heated through and the tomatoes have softened.
6. Top with broken tortilla chips, olives, and the remaining tomatoes and ⅓ cup (85 ml) of cheese. Bake for an additional 10 minutes or until the cheese has melted and the tomatoes are soft.
7. Serve and enjoy.

Seafood Casserole
by Rita DeMontis

CHEESE:
Fontina, Mozzarella, Jarlsberg

PREP   30 minutes

COOK   20–25 minutes

SERVES   8–10

3¼ lb (1.5 kg) large shrimp

12 oz (340 g) firm white fish fillets (such as haddock)

12 oz (340 g) medium scallops

¼ cup + 1 Tbsp (75 ml) sherry, divided

4 cups (1 l) long-grain rice

2 pinches sea salt

¼ cup (60 ml) olive oil

2 Tbsp (30 ml) unsalted butter

½ cup (125 ml) diced green onions, white and green parts

1 clove garlic, minced

1 can (9 oz/255 g) frozen crab meat, thawed

2 Tbsp (30 ml) all-purpose flour

2 cups (500 ml) light cream or whole milk

1 can (10 oz/284 ml) button mushrooms, drained

1 cup (250 ml) frozen baby peas, rinsed under cold water

1 medium field tomato, cored and finely chopped

Freshly ground pepper

¼ cup (60 ml) chopped parsley

1 cup (250 ml) grated fontina cheese, divided

1 cup (250 ml) grated mozzarella cheese, divided

1 cup (250 ml) grated Jarlsberg cheese, divided

1. Preheat the oven to 350°F (180°C).
2. To prepare the shrimp, use your fingers to remove and discard the shells. Using a small sharp knife, make a shallow cut from the top to the bottom along the back portion of the shrimp to expose their digestive tracts. These will look like a black vein. Using the tip of the knife, carefully remove the tract to devein each shrimp. Rinse the prepared shrimp under cold running water, and set aside.
3. Using a large kitchen knife, cut the fish fillets into large chunks.
4. In a large bowl, toss the shrimp, fish, and scallops with ¼ cup (60 ml) of the sherry. Set aside in the refrigerator, covered with plastic wrap, until needed.
5. Combine the rice, 8 cups (2 l) of cold water, and 2 pinches of the sea salt in a large pot over medium heat. Bring to a boil, stir

Rita DeMontis is one of the sweetest women I've ever met. Rita has been the *Toronto Sun* food editor for over 30 years, she has her own radio show, and she is an emcee extraordinaire. With our shared strong Italian roots and passion for food, it was a no brainer that we would become such good friends. She's been so kind to me and my family, and, of course, the shop, too. She always supports my crazy food ideas; whether it's a dinner with a superhero theme or a fundraising barbecue for rescue dogs, she's always first in line to buy a ticket, and she's always there to cover for her strong media following. I'm honored to have one of her recipes for this book. This dish is rich and full of the buttery goodness of cheese. Normally, you wouldn't serve cheese with seafood, but it works beautifully here. You can play with the different seafood options and add a bit more of your favorite. You can also add a bit more cheese, too.

once, and then reduce the heat to low. Cook the rice, covered tightly with a lid, for 6 to 8 minutes or until the rice has absorbed the water and is cooked through. Once cooked, remove it from the heat, and set aside until needed.

6. In a large Dutch oven or pot, heat the olive oil with the butter over medium heat. Sauté the onions and garlic for 4 to 5 minutes or until the onions are no longer opaque. Add the seafood and crab meat, toss well in the hot mixture, and cook for approximately 3 minutes or until the shrimp are pink. Do not overcook. Remove the seafood from the sauce using a slotted spoon, and set aside in a covered dish at room temperature.

7. In the same pot over medium heat, quickly whisk the flour into the sauce to form a roux. Add the rest of the sherry. Slowly whisk in the cream (or milk), and continue whisking until the mixture thickens without bubbling and there are no lumps. Then add the mushrooms, peas, and tomato, and cook, stirring, for 5 minutes or until heated through.

8. Return the seafood to the sauce, and mix well to combine. Add pepper to taste and adjust the seasoning if necessary. Sprinkle with chopped parsley.

9. In a small bowl, blend all the cheeses together. Add 2 cups (500 ml) of the cheese blend to the sauce, sprinkling it 1 handful at a time. Stir to combine, and allow it to melt thoroughly. Reserve some cheese for later.

10. Spray a large lasagna pan with nonstick cooking spray. Add the cooked rice in an even layer on the bottom. Pour the seafood mixture over the rice, and top with the reserved cheese. Cover with aluminum foil, and bake for 20 minutes. Remove the aluminum foil, and on low, broil the top until it is slightly golden and the cheese is bubbly.

11. Serve immediately.

You can omit the rice and toss the seafood mixture in 1 pound (450 g) of hot fettuccini noodles if you prefer.

Stuffed Cheese Pumpkin with Black Rice, Mushrooms, and Cheese
by Daniel Boulud

PREP	30 minutes
COOK	2 hours
SERVES	10–12

1 cheese pumpkin, about 10–12 lb (4.5–5.5 kg)

1 lb (450 g) various wild mushrooms (button, cremini, portobello, etc.)

Sea salt and freshly ground white pepper

½ tsp (2 ml) ground cinnamon

½ tsp (2 ml) ground nutmeg

½ tsp (2 ml) ground ginger

½ tsp (2 ml) ground cloves

1 cup (250 ml) uncooked black rice

2 cups (500 ml) chicken stock

½ cup (125 ml) heavy cream

½ cup (125 ml) toasted and chopped walnuts

½ cup (125 ml) toasted pumpkin seeds

1 bunch chives, sliced

½ lb (225 g) gruyère cheese, grated

1. Preheat the oven to 350°F (180°C), and place a rack in the bottom position.
2. Remove the circular cap of the pumpkin with a small serrated paring knife. Make a hole about 10 inches (25 cm) in diameter, wide enough to fill the pumpkin with stuffing. Remove and discard the seeds and stringy parts of the pumpkin. Reserve the cap.
3. Wash the mushrooms and cut them into 1-inch (2.5 cm) pieces.
4. Sprinkle the inside of the pumpkin with some salt and pepper, as well as cinnamon, nutmeg, ginger, and cloves. Pour the rice, chicken stock, cream, and mushrooms into the pumpkin. Season with salt to taste, and stir the ingredients inside the pumpkin to combine. Return the cap to the pumpkin.

A few years ago, Daniel Boulud, the Michelin-starred, award-winning chef was in Toronto for 2 months putting all the precise finishing touches on his restaurant in the Four Seasons Hotel. One day, Chef Boulud's sous-chef called me to say that his boss needed my assistance. Daniel Boulud needed MY help?! I was shocked, but came right down to the restaurant with everything I could think of to make a dazzling, all-Canadian cheese display. I entered the kitchen, and there he was—the master. He was commanding a huge brigade, but when he saw me, he pointed to a clean prep table right beside him. I knew what that meant: get to work, Afrim. I put my head down and hustled out the most epic cheese display I could do. Chef Boulud worked right beside me, our shoulders touching, and I couldn't help but feel that I was in the presence of true greatness. I'm honored to include Chef Boulud's recipe in my cookbook.

5. Place the pumpkin into the preheated oven, directly on the bottom rack, and bake for 1½ to 2 hours or until the tip of a paring knife can easily pierce the flesh.

6. Carefully remove the pumpkin from the oven and gently remove the cap. Toss the walnuts, pumpkin seeds, chives, and cheese into the pumpkin's rice mixture, and give it a stir using a fork. Check the seasoning, adding more salt if desired. Place the pumpkin back in the oven for 3 to 5 minutes to allow the cheese to melt.

7. Serve the pumpkin warm, using a spoon to scoop a bit of pumpkin from the sides along with the filling. This recipe also makes for a great side dish to your favorite protein.

This Quiche Doesn't Stink

PREP   15 minutes

COOK   45 minutes

SERVES   4

CHEESES:
**Fontina,
Bocconcini**

1 cup (250 ml) spinach

½ cup (125 ml) pine nuts

4 large eggs

¾ cup (185 ml) 35% cream

½ tsp (2 ml) sea salt

¼ tsp (1 ml) cayenne pepper

¼ tsp (1 ml) ground nutmeg

½ tsp (2 ml) dried basil

¼ tsp (1 ml) dried oregano

½ cup (125 ml) grated fontina cheese

3 Tbsp (45 ml) extra-virgin olive oil

1 small white onion, finely chopped

1 clove garlic, finely chopped

1 small green zucchini, thinly sliced

1 small yellow zucchini, thinly sliced

4½ oz (130 g) bocconcini cheese, sliced ⅓ inch (8 mm) thick

3 slightly underripe plum tomatoes, thinly sliced

1 prebaked pie shell (9 inches/23 cm)

4 leaves fresh basil, finely chopped

Most of my staff try to steer clear of Italian fontina cheese because of its stink. When customers ask for it, even I would sometimes rather say, "I'm sorry, we're out of stock." It's that smelly. But, with all that said, Italian fontina is one of a kind, and if you do like big, bold, very pungent cheeses, then definitely try it. Please just come in when I'm not at the shop. Thank you in advance. For this recipe, I prefer to use a local fontina cheese that can be found at most cheese stores. The local fontina cheeses tend to be milder than the Italian kind. They are easier to eat, straightforward, and great for cooking.

1. Preheat the oven to 350°F (180°C).
2. In a medium sauté pan, sauté the spinach (no oil needed) over medium heat for 2 to 3 minutes or until bright green. Remove the spinach from the heat, and allow to cool. Coarsely chop, and set aside.
3. In a small sauté pan, give the pine nuts a gentle toss over medium heat. Evenly toast the pine nuts until golden brown all over—make sure to watch them carefully, because they can burn quickly. Remove them from the heat, and set aside to cool.
4. In a medium mixing bowl, combine the eggs, cream, salt, cayenne pepper, nutmeg, dried basil, oregano, and fontina cheese. Beat the ingredients with an electric mixer for 3 minutes at medium speed, until light and frothy.
5. In a frying pan, heat the extra-virgin olive oil over medium heat. Sauté the onions, garlic, zucchini, and cooked spinach for 3 to 4 minutes or until the vegetables have softened slightly. Remove from the heat.

6. Arrange the bocconcini cheese slices, tomato slices, and sautéed vegetables in the bottom of the pie shell. Pour the egg mixture over the vegetables.
7. Place the quiche into the preheated oven, and bake for 30 minutes or until golden brown. The center of the quiche should have a little jiggle to it when it's done.
8. Remove the quiche from the oven, and garnish with basil and toasted pine nuts.
9. Serve hot.

Deconstructed Cannoli, page 142

DESSERT

138   **Brillat-Savarin with Fresh Strawberries**
        by Jonathan Goodyear

140   **The G.O.A.T. (Greatest of All Time)**

142   **Deconstructed Cannoli**

143   **"I'm Not Afraid of Blue Cheese Anymore"**
        Caramelized Cookies

144   **Grilled Pineapple with Mascarpone**

146   **Olive Oil and Pistachio Cake by Cory Vitiello**

151   **Reggiano the Mighty**

152   **X-Men Ice Cream**

Brillat-Savarin with Fresh Strawberries
by Jonathan Goodyear

PREP 15 minutes
COOK 30 minutes
SERVES 2–4

8 oz (225 g) Brillat-Savarin cheese
1 quart (1 l) fresh local strawberries
½ cup (125 ml) sugar
Seeds from 1 vanilla bean
⅔ cup (165 ml) shelled, toasted, smashed pistachios
Zest from 1 lemon
Grilled baguette, for serving

1. The first step is to always start with a great, well-aged piece of Brillat-Savarin cheese. Remove the cheese from the fridge about 30 minutes before serving, and, using a sharp knife, remove the top rind. The goal is to only remove the rind, exposing the beautiful creamy cheese. This will also allow you to see how the cheese has matured or ripened, and in my opinion, the softer the better!

2. Hull half of the strawberries and leave them whole. Then hull and quarter the other half. In a medium-sized tempered glass mixing bowl, combine the hulled whole strawberries, sugar, and vanilla bean seeds. Toss to coat. Cover with plastic wrap, and place over a heavy-bottomed saucepan filled halfway with water. Bring the water to a boil over high heat, and let the bowl sit over the heat for at least 30 minutes. Make sure the bottom of the bowl isn't touching the water. The heat will help pull all the natural flavor out of the strawberries.

3. Carefully remove the bowl and taste the strawberry liquid. If there is a strong strawberry flavor, then you're ready to remove them from the heat. Pour off and reserve ¼ cup (60 ml) of strawberry juice for later, and set the remaining mixture aside at room temperature. Pour the warmed strawberries and their juices over the quartered strawberries in a medium-sized mixing bowl, and allow to rest for 10 to 15 minutes.

4. Place the cheese in the center of a serving dish, and spoon the strawberries around the cheese. Finish by pouring the reserved strawberry juice and smashed pistachios on top and garnish with grated lemon zest.

5. Serve with grilled bread fresh off the barbecue, and enjoy.

When I first asked Jonathan Goodyear to contribute to this cookbook, he screamed "yes" before he could really think about it. This is pretty much how our friendship works. When I ask for something, "Goody" is always right there. He's been coming to the shop for over 10 years, and for us, food and friendship are always intertwined.

The G.O.A.T.
(Greatest of All Time)

PREP 20 minutes

COOK 3 hours

SERVES 12

CHEESES:
Chèvre des Alpes, Ricotta

4 cups (1 l) finely crushed amaretti cookies

⅓ cup (85 ml) unsalted butter, melted

12 oz (340 g) Chèvre des Alpes goat cheese

1 container (16 oz/450 g) ricotta cheese, room temperature, drained slightly

1 cup (250 ml) superfine granulated sugar

1 tsp (5 ml) vanilla extract

¼ tsp (1 ml) sea salt

4 large eggs, room temperature

1 cup (250 ml) pumpkin purée

½ tsp (2 ml) ground ginger

¼ tsp (1 ml) ground nutmeg

6 oz (170 g) white chocolate, melted

1. Preheat the oven to 325°F (160°C).
2. In a large bowl, mix together the amaretti cookie crumbs and butter using your hands. Be sure to combine well. Press the mixture into the bottom of a 9-inch (23 cm) springform pan.
3. Bake the cookie crumb mixture on the middle rack for 12 minutes or until firm. Remove from the oven, and cool completely at room temperature.
4. Using a stand mixer or a hand-held mixer with a medium bowl, beat the crap out of the Chèvre des Alpes goat cheese for 3 minutes or until it is smooth. Add the ricotta cheese, sugar, vanilla, and salt. Beat for an additional 3 minutes or until mixed well. Add the eggs, 1 at a time, beating well after each addition.
5. Divide the mixture equally between 2 bowls. Fold the pumpkin purée, ginger, and nutmeg into 1 of the bowls, and the melted white chocolate into the other bowl.
6. Pour some of the white chocolate filling into the baked cookie crumb pan to a depth of about ½ inch (about 1.2 cm). Then, a spoonful at a time, alternately add the 2 fillings to fill the pan. Using a spatula, swirl the 2 batters slightly to marbleize.
7. Place the cheesecake, still in the springform pan, on a baking tray.

Imagine a cool autumn day. The trees are bare, leaves are everywhere, and you come inside to a cozy fire, a great cup of tea, and an amazingly rich cheesecake with white chocolate and pumpkin. The star of this recipe and what makes this such a unique cheesecake is the addition of Chèvre des Alpes goat cheese. It adds tang and zip to an already delicious cheesecake. I love goat cheese like this, and I would do anything for it. It's my kryptonite (I hate Superman, but you understand what I'm saying). Always keep a half pound in your fridge, like you would butter.

8. Reduce the oven's temperature to 300°F (150°C). In a separate glass baking dish, pour 2 cups (500 ml) of water, and slide the dish onto the bottom rack of the oven. It will produce steam, which will help the cheesecake stay moist as it bakes. Bake the cheesecake uncovered on the middle rack for 45 minutes. Then turn the oven off, and leave the cheesecake inside the oven for an additional 2 hours, without opening the door. If you are anything like me and have no patience, this will be hard.

9. After 2 hours, remove the cheesecake from the oven and refrigerate it, in its springform pan and covered with aluminum foil, for at least 6 hours before unmolding. I know, 6 hours is a long time, but watch a few episodes of *The Sopranos*, and it will fly by.

Someone told me once if you consume enough nutmeg, it could kill you . . . better go easy on the nutmeg, chef.

Deconstructed Cannoli

PREP	10 minutes
COOK	Nada
SERVES	6–8

1 lb (450 g) fresh ricotta cheese, drained

½ lb (225 g) mascarpone cheese

¾ cup (185 ml) icing sugar

1 tsp (5 ml) ground cinnamon

1 tsp (5 ml) vanilla extract

Zest from 1 medium orange

Juice from ½ medium orange

¼ cup (60 ml) Marsala wine or sweet vermouth

½ cup (125 ml) candied citrus peels (whatever kind you like)

½ cup (125 ml) miniature dark chocolate chips

Cannoli shells, broken into large chunks (see note)

This must be just about the easiest dessert to make, and it has plenty of wow factor. It's a fun, social way to enjoy a classic Italian dessert.

1. Blend the ricotta and mascarpone cheese together in a food processor, along with the icing sugar and cinnamon. Add the vanilla, orange zest, orange juice, and Marsala wine. Blend thoroughly. Add the candied peels and dark chocolate chips, and blend 1 final time to mix well. Transfer the mixture to a decorative glass dish, cover, and refrigerate for up to 30 minutes.

2. Before serving, stir the cheese mixture to freshen. Serve with cannoli chips.

3. This cheese dip will last for up to 5 days, covered, in the refrigerator.

Use store-bought cannoli, cracked into large pieces. You can find cannoli shells at specialty grocery stores or Italian markets. I like to use International Cheese ricotta, carefully drained overnight, for this special dessert.

CHEESE:
Roquefort

Roquefort is one of the most important (and also accidentally made) cheeses of all time. No other blue cheese would have ever existed if it weren't for the Frenchman who discovered what we now know as Roquefort many moons ago. Imagine what soul music would be like without James Brown. Now, as great and important as this blue cheese is, it's still not everyone's cup of tea. Its smell alone can be a little much. So, I have chosen to make a simple recipe with a sweet component that cuts down the intensity of Roquefort, but still lets the cheese sing loud and proud.

"I'm Not Afraid of Blue Cheese Anymore"
Caramelized Cookies

PREP	15 minutes
COOK	5 minutes
SERVES	4–6

12 store-bought shortbread cookies
4 oz (120 g) Roquefort blue cheese, crumbled
2 Tbsp (30 ml) caramel sauce (recipe below or use store-bought)

CARAMEL SAUCE
2 Tbsp (30 ml) sugar
4 tsp (20 ml) salted butter
¼ cup (60 ml) 35% cream

1. Place the cookies on a serving plate, and top with Roquefort blue cheese.
2. To make the caramel sauce, heat the sugar in a small saucepan over medium heat, stirring, for 3 to 4 minutes or until it melts and becomes amber brown. Then quickly add the butter, followed by the cream, and stir for approximately 2 minutes until the sauce is smooth. Keep in mind that the sugar will foam up when you add the butter and cream. Remove the saucepan from the heat, and transfer the sauce to a bowl. Allow it to cool for a couple of minutes before using.
3. Drizzle the warm caramel sauce over the cheese on the cookies. Serve, tout de suite!

There are many grades of Roquefort cheese. When buying, look at it as though you are buying a Mercedes. Whether it's the E-Class or the S-Class, it's still a Mercedes—you can't really go wrong.

Grilled Pineapple
with Mascarpone

PREP	20 minutes
COOK	3 minutes
SERVES	6

1 pineapple

1 tsp (5 ml) vanilla extract

1 (16 oz/450 g) store-bought tub mascarpone cheese

½ cup (125 ml) brown sugar

3 Tbsp (45 ml) freshly squeezed orange juice

1 Tbsp (15 ml) unsalted butter, melted

1 tsp (5 ml) ground cinnamon

Agave nectar, for drizzling

1. Preheat the barbecue to 400°F (200°C), or a grill pan over medium heat.
2. Using a sharp knife, peel and core the pineapple. Cut the pineapple flesh into 1-inch-thick (2.5 cm) half-moons, and set them aside at room temperature.
3. Pour the vanilla into the tub of mascarpone cheese. Give it a gentle stir, and set aside.
4. In a small bowl, mix the sugar, orange juice, butter, and cinnamon together. Brush each of the pineapple pieces with this mixture.
5. Grill the pineapple for approximately 1 minute on each side or until they brown.
6. Transfer the grilled pineapple to a serving platter, and top each slice with 2 large tablespoons of the mascarpone cheese. Finish with a drizzle of agave nectar.

I'm going to be honest with you; I'm not a huge lover of mascarpone (and a hush goes over the crowd). But it works perfectly in this recipe. Besides putting it in desserts, I find mascarpone to be pretty useless (tell us how you really feel, Afrim). And, as it happens, I feel the same way about pineapple. I unfriend people who put pineapple on their pizza. So, let's see how I can take 2 ingredients that I'm not very fond of and make them taste like magic. Despite all the food bashing here, I promise this recipe rocks, but just make sure to use *all* the mascarpone and pineapple because you aren't allowed to do anything with the leftovers, like putting them on pizza.

Olive Oil and Pistachio Cake
by Cory Vitiello

PREP   30 minutes
COOK   30–40 minutes
SERVES   8

CHEESE:
Goat

Pistachio and Olive Oil Cake

Unsalted butter, for greasing

2 large eggs

2 egg yolks

⅔ cup (165 ml) sugar

1½ tsp (7 ml) ground cinnamon

½ cup (125 ml) cornmeal

1 tsp (5 ml) baking powder

Grated zest and juice from 1 fresh lemon

1 cup (250 ml) finely ground pistachios (store-bought or ground
    in a food processor)

¾ cup (185 ml) whole milk

1 cup (250 ml) extra-virgin olive oil

1¾ cups (440 ml) all-purpose flour

1. Preheat the oven to 325°F (160°C), and prepare a 9-inch
   (23 cm) loaf pan by greasing it with unsalted butter.

2. Place the eggs, egg yolks, and sugar in the bowl of a stand
   mixer, and whip on high speed for roughly 3 minutes or until
   the mixture triples in volume. Turn the mixer to low, and add
   the cinnamon, cornmeal, baking powder, lemon zest and juice,
   and ground pistachios. Continue mixing until well
   incorporated. In a slow drizzle, pour in the milk and olive oil,
   and mix until incorporated. With the mixer on low speed, sift in
   the flour and fold it into the batter. Take care not to overmix
   once the flour is in or the final cake won't be as delicate as
   you'd like it to be.

3. Pour the batter into the prepared loaf pan, cover with
   aluminum foil, and place in the oven, on the middle rack. Bake
   for 30 to 40 minutes or until just cooked in the center. The cake
   should still be very moist in the middle. Remove the cake from
   the oven, and allow it to cool in the pan before removing.

This is my boy, my partner in crime, one of my best friends on the planet, Cory Vitiello. Here is a list of things we've done together to solidify what I feel is the ultimate Toronto culinary bromance:

- We frequent Yogurty's and Bed Bath & Beyond (don't judge us).
- We love *The Bachelor* and all other affiliated TV shows involving useless, over-the-top drama.
- We've traveled together (we had the best tasting menu at Burger King in Boston).
- We enjoy lazy Sundays driving around looking at nice houses.

Beyond being ridiculously tall and insanely handsome, he's one of the most technical chefs I've ever met. His food is simple, it's straightforward, and you always want to dive right into it. He also makes some of the best desserts I've ever had. Here is Cory's olive oil and pistachio cake with whipped goat cheese, poached rhubarb, and crunchy meringue. My boy has mad skills and I got lots of love for him.

Whipped Goat Cheese

7 oz (200 g) goat cheese, room temperature
2 Tbsp (30 ml) heavy cream
2 Tbsp (30 ml) honey
Grated zest and juice from ½ fresh lemon

1. Place the cheese, cream, honey, and lemon zest and juice in the bowl of a stand mixer with the whisk attachment, and blend on high speed for 1 minute or until smooth and creamy. Take care not to overmix.
2. Transfer the mixture to a small bowl, and keep at room temperature until ready to use. If made in advance, store in the refrigerator in an airtight container, but allow it to come back to room temperature before serving.

Poached Rhubarb

4 cups (1 l) rhubarb, diced in ½-inch-thick (1.2 cm) slices
Grated zest and juice from 1 fresh lemon
⅓ cup (85 ml) sugar
⅓ cup (85 ml) honey

1. Place the rhubarb, 1½ cups (375 ml) of water, the lemon zest and juice, sugar, and honey in a small stainless-steel saucepan over low heat. Cook, stirring occasionally, for 10 minutes or until the rhubarb is just tender. Allow the rhubarb to cool in the juices.

Crunchy Meringue

4 egg whites
1½ tsp (7 ml) ground ginger
1¾ cups (440 ml) icing sugar

1. Preheat the oven to 200°F (95°C), and line a baking sheet with parchment paper.
2. Place the egg whites and ginger in the bowl of a stand mixer with the whisk attachment, and turn to medium-high speed. When the egg whites just begin to foam, start sprinkling in the sugar, a little bit at a time. The egg whites will begin to take on more volume. Stop beating when they stiffen up and take on a shiny, smooth appearance.

Continued over

3. Transfer the meringue to the prepared baking sheet, and using a straight spatula, smooth it out to a thin consistent layer. Place the meringue in the oven and use a wooden spoon to prop the door slightly open. Bake the meringue for 3 hours or until it's fully dried.

4. The meringue can be baked the morning or day before baking the cake if you have only 1 oven. If you make it ahead of time, store the meringue tightly wrapped at room temperature.

Garnish

Olive oil, for drizzling
Mint leaves
Cracked pistachios

1. To serve, place a piece of the cake onto each plate and serve with a dollop of whipped goat cheese, a large spoonful of the poached rhubarb and its juices, and a few large wafers of the crunchy meringue. Garnish with a drizzle of olive oil, mint leaves, and cracked pistachios.

CHEESE:
Parmigiano-Reggiano

Reggiano **the Mighty**

PREP	7 minutes
COOK	N/A
SERVES	6–8

4 cups (1 l) fresh, locally grown strawberries, hulled and halved
⅓ cup (85 ml) balsamic vinegar
3 Tbsp (45 ml) extra-virgin olive oil
2 Tbsp (30 ml) flaked sea salt
1 Tbsp (15 ml) freshly ground pepper
10½ oz (300 g) Parmigiano-Reggiano cheese, room temperature

1. In a large metal bowl, gently toss the strawberries with the balsamic vinegar and olive oil. You will want to take it easy on these nice, ripe strawberries. Add the salt and pepper, and give another gentle toss.
2. Cover the bowl with plastic wrap or aluminum foil, and freeze for 5 minutes, or if you have the time, refrigerate for 1 hour.
3. Break off nice, big chunks of Parmigiano-Reggiano cheese, and place them on a serving plate or marble slab, or even in your hand.
4. Take the now infused strawberries, and pour everything right over the hunks of the cheese. There's no turning back now. Especially if you're holding a big handful of Reggiano.
5. The objective is to have the cheese and strawberries together in 1 delicious bite.

Reggiano is truly the king of all cheeses. I'm sorry to all the other great cheeses in this book, and to all the others that are made across the globe, but Reggiano rules! Made in Parma, Italy, it's practically currency in that country. There are really no other cheeses like it. A nice big hunk of Reggiano can act as a baby pacifier too—just ask Mrs. and Mr. Pristine. This recipe is truly a rustic classic. Buy the best-quality ingredients you can afford, let them shine in this savory and tart dessert, and let's all pay respect to the king.

When shopping for balsamic vinegar, go to a high-end specialty food store and ask for the good stuff. It's important to get a nicely aged balsamic vinegar from Modena, Italy. Ten to 15 years old is ideal, or if you want to show off to your friends, buy a 25-year-old balsamic. Don't use your everyday, workhorse olive oil. Get something midrange, and it should be light and fruity. When it comes to the Parmigiano-Reggiano cheese, buy a big piece—bigger than your hand but smaller than your head, or just ask for what I suggest at your local cheese shop.

X-Men Ice Cream

PREP 10 minutes

COOK 15 minutes, plus 4 hours for freezing

SERVES 4

CHEESES:
**Cream Cheese,
Mimolette**

5 plum tomatoes

½ cup (125 ml) sugar

½ tsp (2 ml) vanilla extract

¼ tsp (1 ml) ground cinnamon

¾ cup (185 ml) cream cheese

⅓ cup (85 ml) whole milk

2 cups (500 ml) vanilla ice cream, softened

2 oz (60 g) finely grated mimolette cheese, divided

1. In a large saucepan, bring 4 cups (1 l) of cold water to a boil over medium-high heat. Lightly score an X (for "X-Men Ice Cream") in the bottom of each tomato, and cook the tomatoes for 2 minutes or until softened. Transfer the tomatoes to a bowl of cold water. Carefully remove the skins, stems, and seeds, and dice the flesh. Discard the extra cold tomato water or use it to make a Caesar or Bloody Mary.

2. In the same saucepan, combine the tomato flesh, sugar, vanilla, and cinnamon over medium heat. Mix well to combine the flavors. Simmer for 10 minutes or until the liquid becomes syrupy. Remove from the heat, and cool at room temperature.

3. In a medium bowl, stir the cream cheese with a wooden spoon to soften it while adding the milk. Gradually add the ice cream. Stir until completely smooth, and then gently stir in the tomato mixture.

4. Cover the bowl with aluminum foil, and place it into the freezer for at least 4 hours before serving.

5. When you are ready to indulge, scoop the ice cream into 4 serving bowls, and top each with a quarter of the grated mimolette cheese.

This recipe is meant to be eaten in the summer months, when the tomatoes are at their tastiest and when you want to eat gallons and gallons of ice cream. I was inspired to create this by the chefs who led the molecular gastronomy movement—Ferran Adrià, René Redzepi, and Grant Achatz. These chefs and many others manipulated top-notch ingredients to create truly mind-blowing dishes. I often teach cheese workshops, and during the heyday of molecular gastronomy, I played around with liquid nitrogen to create a quick cheese ice cream. My father wasn't impressed with my laissez-faire attitude toward safety (I made this ice cream with a huge canister of liquid nitrogen in the passenger seat of our Cheese Boutique delivery van on the way to an event . . . I was basically a ticking time bomb), but I'm happy to say it worked out— and I've now come up with a much safer method.

Oysters Gouda, Hold the Rockefeller, page 169

SNACKS

157   1, 2, 3 Strikes You're Out Muffins

158   The Ardiana Grilled Cheese

160   Afrim is Cuckoo for Kaltbach

161   Fruity, Cheesy Gazpacho, Por Favor

163   Creamy Fromage and Biscotti

164   Embrace the Stinky Bread

166   The Meatless Wheatless Pizza

167   "How Do You Like D'em Apples?" Bars

168   Matty's Game Day Dip by Matt Dean Pettit

169   Oysters Gouda, Hold the Rockefeller

170   Polenta Arancini by Massimo Capra

173   Stuffed Turkey Meatballs Matt Damon–Style

174   "You're So Vain" Pesto

CHEESE:
Lemon Stilton

I'm about to throw you a curveball of Sandy Koufax–like proportions with this recipe. It's a grand slam. Blue stilton is one of the most important cheeses ever to be created. There are so many other blue cheeses made around the world, but they all emulate the pungent blue from England. Lemon stilton is its lesser-known cousin, but it's worth hunting down for this recipe. The classic blue veins are replaced with lemon chunks and zest, and it works wonderfully for this dish.

1, 2, 3 Strikes You're Out
Muffins

PREP	10 minutes
COOK	25 minutes
MAKES	12 muffins

1 cup (250 ml) all-purpose flour

1 cup (250 ml) whole wheat flour

1 cup (250 ml) crumbled lemon stilton cheese (or substitute white stilton)

⅔ cup (165 ml) quick cooking rolled oats, divided

2 tsp (10 ml) baking powder

½ tsp (2 ml) baking soda

½ tsp (2 ml) fine sea salt

1 large egg

1¼ cups (310 ml) buttermilk

¾ cup (185 ml) packed brown sugar, divided

¼ cup (60 ml) unsalted butter, melted, plus extra for greasing

2 tsp (10 ml) vanilla extract

1 cup (250 ml) chopped fresh local strawberries

1. Preheat the oven to 375°F (190°C).
2. Grease a 12-cup nonstick muffin pan with unsalted butter.
3. In a large bowl, combine the flours, lemon stilton cheese, ½ cup (125 ml) of the oats, baking powder, baking soda, and sea salt. Mix well.
4. In another bowl, whisk together the egg, buttermilk, ⅔ cup (165 ml) of the brown sugar, melted butter, and vanilla.
5. Pour the wet ingredients into the dry ingredients, all at once, and lightly incorporate with a whisk. Gently stir in the strawberries.
6. Spoon the batter into the prepared muffin pan, and use the back of a spoon to smooth out the tops. Sprinkle each muffin with a pinch each of the remaining oats and brown sugar.
7. Place the muffins into the preheated oven, and bake for approximately 25 minutes or until the tops are firm to the touch.
8. Let the muffins cool in the pan for 10 minutes or so. Take the muffins out of the pan, and enjoy. These will keep, sealed in an airtight container and refrigerated, for 3 days.

The Ardiana Grilled Cheese

PREP   10 minutes
COOK   8 minutes
SERVES 2

1 medium banana

4 slices white bread (or whatever bread suits your fancy)

2 oz (60 g) Danish or locally made havarti cheese, sliced ¼ inch
(6 mm) thick

1 oz (30 g) milk or dark chocolate, coarsely chopped

2 tsp (10 ml) unsalted butter, softened

1. Using a sharp knife, cut the banana into thin slices lengthwise.
   Set aside.
2. Preheat a medium skillet over medium heat.
3. Place 2 slices of bread on a work surface. Evenly cover each
   slice with a piece of havarti cheese. Divide the chocolate and
   banana slices, and place them overtop of the cheese. Close the
   sandwiches with the remaining 2 bread slices.
4. Spread butter on the outside of the sandwiches and gently
   place the sandwiches in the skillet.
5. Cook the sandwiches for 3 to 4 minutes per side, flipping once,
   or until the bread is golden brown and the cheese has melted.
6. Cut the grilled cheeses into 4 squares, and serve while hot.

Believe it or not, I had never
tasted havarti cheese until a
few years ago. I don't know
why I decided that I didn't like
it, but I somehow managed to
avoid tasting it for decades—
and I taste 30 to 50 cheeses a
day. At some point, I think it
became an inner challenge to
see how long I could hold out.
I caved when my 16-year-old
niece, Ardiana, gave me a big
hunk of havarti for my birthday
as a joke, all the while knowing
my relationship with the
cheese. But she had just started
working at the store, and I
didn't want to let her down
and seem unthankful. So I ate
it. It was enjoyable and I moved
on. To make up for hating
havarti all these years, I decided
to give it some love in this
cookbook (grudgingly, of
course).

Afrim Is Cuckoo for Kaltbach

PREP	Not much because I know how busy you are
COOK	None
SERVES	As many people as you want to share with

CHEESE:
**Kaltbach
Gruyère**

A big piece of Kaltbach gruyère cheese (be sure to get this particular one, or else)

A chilled bottle of good riesling

1. Remove the gruyère cheese from the refrigerator and bring to room temperature about 1 hour before serving.
2. Eat the cheese.
3. In the same mouthful, drink the wine. Swallow.
4. Repeat a few hundred times.

Years ago, when I was making cheese in Switzerland, I had the privilege of visiting the home of the best gruyère cheese, the Kaltbach Mountain in the region of Fribourg. The Swiss Cheese Association welcomed me into their private cheese caves like Batman welcomed Robin, and this visit was perhaps the most important cheese moment of my life. The cave itself is damp, dank, moldy, cold, and humid. And the cheese absolutely loves these conditions. I had to wear a full hazmat suit before going in (seriously), because not even an inch of skin can be exposed to the air. And even with that protection, I couldn't help but tear up because of all the funk and ammonia smells emanating throughout the cave (or that may be just me and my cheesy tears of joy). This is considered "controlled mold." Once I began trying the Kaltbach gruyère cheese, I ate it like it was going out of style. The flavor is so complex—it's fruity, nutty, bold, and creamy. So much is happening with this cheese, and we have the most gnarly cave to thank for it, that I like to serve it simply on its own.

Cotija cheese (pronounced "ko-TEE-ha") is the quintessential taco cheese in Mexico. It's a fresh cow's milk cheese with very little flavor other than salt. It's versatile and a staple in authentic Mexican cuisine. It grates well, it crumbles well, and it can make a dish pop. Think of this cheese as similar to feta, but without as much moisture. It's meant to be dry and salty, which is why it works so well grated on tacos. Now, imagine you are in your backyard. You've just made a big batch of chicken tacos, you are wearing your favorite sombrero, and you're ready to dance the mariachi. All of which means that you're ready to make some cheesy gazpacho.

Fruity, Cheesy Gazpacho, Por Favor

PREP	30 minutes plus 2 hours for refrigeration
COOK	N/A
SERVES	6–8 caballeros

½ medium white onion, coarsely chopped
1 medium red bell pepper, coarsely chopped
2 cups (500 ml) hulled and coarsely chopped strawberries
1 cup (250 ml) pitted and coarsely chopped cherries
1 cup (250 ml) diced peaches
1 cup (250 ml) raspberries
1–2 Tbsp (15–30 ml) honey
1 Tbsp (15 ml) white balsamic vinegar
Freshly ground pepper
1½ Tbsp (25 ml) extra-virgin olive oil
3 Tbsp (45 ml) fresh basil, coarsely chopped
4 oz (120 g) cotija cheese, crumbled

1. In a food processor, purée the onion and red bell pepper. Transfer to a large bowl.
2. Add the strawberries, cherries, peaches, and raspberries to the puréed mixture. Stir to combine. Add the honey and balsamic vinegar. Season to taste with pepper. Cover the bowl with plastic wrap and refrigerate for approximately 2 hours to allow the flavors to combine.
3. Remove the bowl from the refrigerator, and stir in the olive oil. Divide the gazpacho into glass dishes, and garnish with fresh basil and cotija cheese. Serve immediately.

Creamy Fromage
and Biscotti

PREP	10 minutes
COOK	1 episode of *Dexter* (50 minutes)
MAKES	48 biscotti

This triple cream brie from the Agropur Signature line of cheeses is a cow's milk cheese produced in Quebec. It's super-rich, fatty, and perfectly salty. It's fairly mild mannered and not offensively pungent like some of the other stinkers in this book. Please give this cheese 2 to 3 hours at room temperature before consuming. Like a fine red wine, this cheese needs to breathe and open up. Also, spoil yourself and get some good Champagne (or sparkling wine will do). Triple cream brie + biscotti + Champagne = #sofriggingood.

5 oz (140 g) triple cream brie, plus extra for serving
2¾ cups (680 ml) all-purpose flour
2 tsp (10 ml) baking powder
1 tsp (5 ml) fine sea salt
1 tsp (5 ml) freshly ground pepper
6 dried figs, finely chopped
10 dried apricots, finely chopped
½ cup (125 ml) raw, skinless, unsalted whole almonds
⅓ cup (85 ml) 2% milk
¼ cup (60 ml) extra-virgin olive oil
3 large eggs

1. Preheat the oven to 350°F (180°C), and line a baking sheet with parchment paper.
2. Break up the brie with your fingers into bite-sized chunks. In a large bowl, sift together the flour, baking powder, and salt. Stir in the pepper, cheese, dried fruit, and almonds. Set aside at room temperature.
3. In a separate small bowl, whisk together the milk, olive oil, and eggs.
4. Fold the wet ingredients into the dry ingredients, all at once. Then knead the dough. Get your knuckles really in there, and beat the crap out of it. When you're done, it should look like a coarse paste. Divide the dough in half and shape each piece into 2½- × 12-inch (7 × 30 cm) logs. Place the logs at least 6 inches (15 cm) apart on the prepared baking sheet.
5. Bake the logs for 25 to 30 minutes or until lightly browned and firm. Remove them from the oven, and cool at room temperature for approximately 10 minutes.
6. Meanwhile, reduce the oven's temperature to 325°F (160°C).
7. Using a serrated knife, cut each log on the diagonal into ¼-inch (6 mm) slices. Return the cut biscotti to the baking sheet, flat side up, and bake for approximately 20 minutes, flipping the biscotti halfway, or until the almonds are lightly toasted and the biscotti are dry. Remove from the oven, and allow to cool. Serve with additional brie. These will keep in a lidded glass jar, at room temperature, for a few months.

Embrace the Stinky Bread

PREP	10 minutes
COOK	30 minutes
SERVES	4 (or 1 hungry Afrim)

CHEESE:
Appenzeller

SALSA VERDE

1 clove garlic, coarsely chopped

½ small white onion, coarsely chopped

1 small jalapeño pepper, seeded

½ cup (125 ml) cilantro

1 can (28 oz/796 ml) whole tomatillos, drained

Juice from 1 fresh lime

Fine sea salt

1½ lb (700 g) round loaf of sourdough rye bread

10 oz (285 g) grated Appenzeller cheese

1. Preheat the oven to 375°F (190°C), and line a baking sheet with parchment paper.
2. To make the salsa verde, combine the garlic, onion, jalapeño, and cilantro in a food processor. Process the ingredients until finely chopped. Add the tomatillos, and pulse until combined, but don't pulse the living daylights out of it; be sure to leave some texture. Mix in the lime juice, and season to taste with salt. Should you have any leftover salsa verde, transfer it to an airtight container, and refrigerate for up to 5 days.
3. To assemble, place the loaf of bread on the prepared baking sheet.
4. Using a knife, make cuts 2 inches (5 cm) deep and 1 inch (2.5 cm) apart in the loaf. Rotate the loaf a quarter-turn, and make the same cuts again to create 1-inch (2.5 cm) cubes.
5. Pour some salsa verde into each of the cuts. Then take the cheese and stuff it into each of the cuts. Cover the loaf with aluminum foil, and bake for approximately 20 minutes. Remove the foil, and bake for an additional 7 minutes or until golden brown and the cheese has melted.
6. Serve hot, and tear this cheesy bread to shreds.

I love using Appenzeller cheese when cooking because of its melting properties and the distinctive aroma it gives off when it's melted. Imagine a beautiful summer day on a dairy farm in Appenzell, Switzerland. Flowers are blossoming, and the lush vegetation all around you is waving in a slight breeze. There's a beautiful scent in the air and then a cow comes along and passes some gas. That's exactly what your house will smell like after you make this recipe. I call that "pleasant pungentness."

The **Meatless Wheatless** Pizza

PREP   10 minutes
COOK   15 minutes
SERVES   4

4 portobello mushrooms

Extra-virgin olive oil for drizzling and greasing

2 medium plum tomatoes, finely diced

¼ cup (60 ml) finely chopped black olives

1 handful fresh spinach

Fine sea salt and freshly ground pepper

7 oz (200 g) fresh mozzarella cheese, coarsely chopped

1. Preheat the oven to 350°F (180°C).
2. Gently clean the mushrooms using a moist paper towel. Cut the stems off each, and set aside at room temperature.
3. Lightly grease a baking sheet with olive oil.
4. In a small bowl, carefully toss together the tomatoes, olives, and spinach, and drizzle with olive oil.
5. Lightly sprinkle the mushroom caps with salt and pepper. Place the caps, gill side up, on the prepared baking sheet. Evenly spoon the tomato mixture onto the mushroom caps, and top with mozzarella cheese.
6. Place the mushroom caps into the preheated oven, and bake for approximately 15 minutes or until the mushrooms are cooked and the cheese is melted. Serve immediately.

CHEESE:
Fresh Mozzarella (Fior Di Latte)

Even the most carnivorous of all carnivores will like this recipe. It's simple, it's straightforward, and believe it or not, it's meaty. In my professional (and personal) opinion, you can't make pizza without fresh cow's milk mozzarella, or fior di latte, as the Italians call it. It's made locally all over North America and can be imported as well. I usually call my good friend, Uncle Dominik, at International Cheese Company in Toronto for the good stuff, and you can also find his cheeses all across Canada.

CHEESE:
**Applewood
Cheddar**

Applewood cheddar is a
traditional farmhouse cheese
that is produced by Ilchester
Cheese Company in Somerset,
England. It's creamy and bold,
and full of smoky goodness. It's
as if an awesome smoky bacon
met a sharp, full-flavored
cheddar. I've never been a big
fan of cheddar (don't judge
me) but this is a tasty cheese
that is great to cook with.
Beyond these sweet and savory
power bars, this cheese is also
delicious melted on a burger.

"How Do You Like D'em Apples?" Bars

PREP	20 minutes
COOK	30 minutes
MAKES	16 bars

½ cup (125 ml) unsalted butter, room temperature, plus extra to
   grease the pan
2 cups (500 ml) all-purpose flour
¼ cup (60 ml) sugar
1 tsp (5 ml) baking powder
6 oz (170 g) shredded Applewood cheddar cheese
1 cup (250 ml) apple jelly
3 Tbsp (45 ml) chopped unsalted pistachios

1. Preheat the oven to 350°F (180°C). Grease a 9-inch-square
   (23 cm) baking pan with butter.
2. In a food processor or a stand mixer, pulse the flour, butter, sugar,
   baking powder, Applewood cheddar cheese, and 2 teaspoons
   (10 ml) of lukewarm water until the mixture is crumbly.
3. Press half of the dough mixture into the baking pan. Spread the
   apple jelly overtop of the crust.
4. Stir the pistachios into the remaining half of the dough, and then
   spread it evenly over the apple jelly. Press down gently. Bake on
   the middle rack of the oven for 30 minutes or until golden brown.
5. Remove the baking pan from the oven and cool on the counter
   for 20 minutes. Cut into bars.
6. Store in an airtight container in the fridge for up to 7 days.

Matty's Game Day Dip
by Matt Dean Pettit

PREP   35 minutes

COOK   3–4 hours

SERVES   4–6

CHEESES:
Cream Cheese, Ricotta

2 live lobsters (1½ lb/700 g each)

1 medium Spanish onion, finely diced

1 small jalapeño, seeded and finely diced

1 Tbsp (15 ml) Old Bay Seasoning (or seafood seasoning of your choice)

Grated zest and juice from 1 fresh lemon, divided

1 cup (250 ml) plain brick-style cream cheese

1 cup (250 ml) good-quality ricotta cheese

½ cup (125 ml) 14% sour cream

1 tsp (5 ml) smoked paprika

½ bunch flat-leaf parsley, chiffonaded

Kosher salt and pepper

French baguette, sourdough bread, or your favorite crackers, for serving

---

Matt Dean Pettit isn't just a fellow cookbook author or friend. He's also my personal Aquaman, my ally in the pursuit of culinary perfection. Slow cooker or crock pot recipes are some of my favorites. This method of cooking is perfect for when you want to relax, put your feet up, and watch the big game. And this lobster recipe from the lobster king, MDP, is perfect for any cheese lover.

1. Prepare an ice bath in a large bowl or the sink.

2. Bring a large pot of 24 cups (6 l) of water to a boil over high heat. Using tongs, submerge the lobsters head first into the pot, and boil for 8 to 10 minutes or until they turn bright red. Carefully remove the lobsters from the boiling water, and plunge them into the ice bath. Let them rest there for 5 to 10 minutes.

3. Using your kitchen tools, crack the shells of the lobsters and remove all the meat, discarding the shells. Coarsely chop the meat, and set aside.

4. Turn your slow cooker on high.

5. Place the onion and jalapeño in the slow cooker, and sweat for 12 to 15 minutes or until soft. Add the Old Bay Seasoning, lemon juice, cream cheese, ricotta cheese, sour cream, lobster meat, and paprika. Stir well to ensure there are no large chunks. Fold in the parsley and lemon zest. Season to taste with salt and pepper.

6. Reduce the heat to low, and cook for 3 to 4 hours, stirring occasionally, or until the cheese is bubbly and starting to turn brown.

7. Serve hot in large bowls paired with cut pieces of fresh French baguette or other option.

Oysters Gouda,
Hold the Rockefeller

PREP	15 minutes
COOK	3 minutes
SERVES	4

2 Tbsp (30 ml) dried herbes de Provence

Grated zest from 1 fresh lemon

½ cup (125 ml) fine breadcrumbs

½ cup (125 ml) melted unsalted butter

12 fresh oysters

12 thin slices aged gouda cheese

1. Preheat the barbecue to 350°F (180°C).
2. In a medium bowl, combine the herbes de Provence, lemon zest, and breadcrumbs. Add the melted butter, and stir well to combine. Set aside at room temperature.
3. Run the oysters under cold water, and use a brush to remove any grit. Then, using an oyster knife, run it along the hinge of the shell, inserting it at the center and giving a slight twist to pop the shell open, leaving the oyster attached on the bottom. If you're nervous about shucking oysters and if you ask nicely, I'm sure your fishmonger will do it for you.
4. Turn the oysters over on a baking sheet to drain off the excess liquor (a.k.a. oyster juice). Set the drained oysters aside on a cutting board, and discard the liquor. Then return the oysters to the baking sheet, meat side up.
5. Top the drained oysters evenly with the herb mixture, then add a slice of aged gouda cheese on top of each. You want the cheese to perfectly cover the oyster, so trim if you need to.
6. Transfer the baking sheet with the oysters onto the grill and close the lid. Cook for approximately 3 minutes or until the cheese is melted and bubbling.

I adore aged gouda, from the Netherlands or even made locally. Hook me up, please! This cheese is nutty and sharp, and when it's melted, the flavor completely changes into something like a butterscotch or warm caramel. In many cuisines, it's a big fat NO-NO to combine fish and cheese, but I disagree, and this recipe shows why. Of course seafood can overpower cheese sometimes, and vice versa, but as long as you have balanced flavors when you combine the ingredients, you'll be okay. You don't want them to compete, but rather complement and play off one another (Joe Montana to Jerry Rice, anyone?).

Polenta Arancini
by Massimo Capra

PREP	20 minutes
COOK	45–50 minutes
SERVES	2–4

2 tsp (10 ml) fine sea salt

1¾ cups (440 ml) polenta (yellow cornmeal)

2 medium egg yolks

3 green onions, white and green parts, finely chopped

⅓ cup (85 ml) finely chopped sun-dried tomatoes

1½ cups (375 ml) grated Parmigiano-Reggiano cheese

Freshly ground pepper

3 cups (750 ml) finely chopped cremini mushrooms

1 clove garlic, finely chopped

1 tsp (5 ml) extra-virgin olive oil

2 cups (500 ml) diced fontina cheese

¼ cup (60 ml) vegetable oil

2 medium eggs, beaten

2 cups (500 ml) fine breadcrumbs

1. Bring 6 cups (1.5 l) of water to a boil in a large copper pot or saucepan over high heat. Add the salt, and then gradually whisk in the polenta, stirring often. Reduce the heat to low, and cook for approximately 40 minutes or until the mixture thickens and the polenta is tender. Pour the soft-cooked polenta directly on a wooden board to cool. All the liquid should have been absorbed at this point. Set aside at room temperature.

2. In a bowl, combine 4 cups (1 l) of the cooked polenta with the egg yolks, green onions, sun-dried tomatoes, and Parmigiano-Reggiano cheese. Season to taste with salt and pepper. Mix well.

Massimo Capra may be best known as a celebrity chef with a famous mustache, but underneath his impressive facial hair is an absolute gentleman with a wealth of Italian food knowledge. I don't think I've ever met a chef who loves and appreciates food like Massimo does. To hear him talk with his unique northern Italian accent about anything food related is inspiring and always makes me hungry. He has worked at many of the top Italian restaurants in Canada, and currently has his own spot just outside of Toronto called Capra's Kitchen. If you want to eat well and have a great night, go visit Massimo. The smells from the kitchen and his huge, jovial personality can fill any room.

 If you are using leftover polenta, skip the first step.

3. In a sauté pan, sauté the mushrooms with the garlic in the extra-virgin olive oil for approximately 5 minutes or until the mushrooms are soft. Let cool, and add the fontina cheese, stirring to combine.

4. Using an ice cream scoop, take a portion of the polenta mixture and shape it, by hand, into a ball. Flatten it in the palm of your hand, add a healthy spoonful of the mushroom filling to the center of it, and fold the flattened polenta over to form a shell around the filling. Repeat until the polenta and stuffing are used up. Set aside at room temperature.

5. In a deep pan over medium heat, bring the vegetable oil to 350°F (180°C). Make sure the oil reaches temperature so the arancini don't fall apart.

6. Dredge each polenta ball in the beaten egg mixture, followed by the breadcrumbs until coated. Shallow-fry, in batches, for 8 to 10 minutes or until golden brown. Do not overfill the pan, and make sure the oil comes back up to temperature between batches.

7. Drain the polenta arancini on a plate lined with paper towel to absorb any excess oil. Transfer to a serving platter, and serve warm.

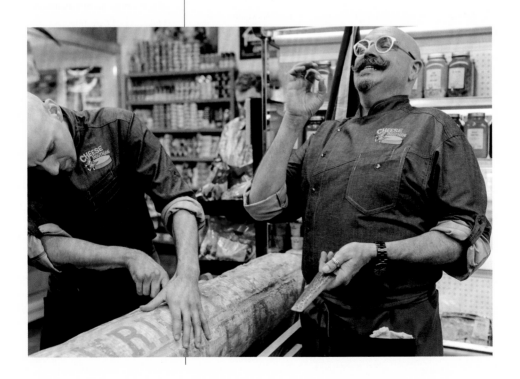

CHEESE:
Mozzarella

Stuffed Turkey Meatballs
Matt Damon–Style

PREP	30 minutes
COOK	10 minutes
SERVES	6

5 oz (140 g) mozzarella cheese

1 lb (450 g) lean ground turkey

½ cup (125 ml) fine breadcrumbs

1 large egg

2 green onions, white and green parts, thinly sliced

2 cloves garlic, finely chopped

1 tsp (5 ml) dried thyme

1 tsp (5 ml) dried oregano

Pinch of fine sea salt and freshly ground pepper

⅓ cup (85 ml) extra-virgin olive oil

¾ cup (185 ml) store-bought medium-spicy salsa

¾ cup (185 ml) puréed jarred tomatoes

Grated zest and juice from 1 lime

It is always a great idea to keep a pound of plain mozzarella cheese in your fridge. When you are in a rush, or smack-dab in the middle of a cheese dilemma, reach for the mozzarella. It's straightforward, tasty, easy to find in grocery stores, and, most importantly for me, one of the best melting cheeses ever. I consider mozzarella the Matt Damon of melting cheeses. Just like Matt, mozzarella is versatile, mild in flavor, and a bit dreamy. Now, if you'll excuse me, I'm off to re-watch *The Talented Mr. Ripley* and the entire Bourne series.

1. Using a sharp knife, cut the mozzarella cheese into ½-inch (1.2 cm) cubes to make 18 evenly sized pieces. Set aside at room temperature.

2. In a large bowl, combine the turkey, breadcrumbs, egg, green onions, garlic, thyme, oregano, and salt and pepper. Mix gently with your hands.

3. Taking 1 tablespoon (15 ml) at a time, shape the meat mixture into 18 balls and bury a cube of cheese in the middle of each ball.

4. In a medium nonstick skillet, heat the olive oil over high heat.

5. Fry the meatballs in the hot oil for approximately 10 minutes, shaking the pan so the meatballs brown evenly. Transfer the meatballs to a plate lined with paper towel to drain any excess oil.

6. In a small bowl, combine the salsa, puréed tomatoes, and lime zest and juice.

7. Serve the meatballs on a large platter with a side of salsa dip, and don't forget to cue up *Good Will Hunting*.

"You're So Vain" Pesto

PREP   15 minutes

COOK   3 minutes

MAKES   2 cups (500 ml)

⅓ cup (85 ml) cashew nuts

1 cup (250 ml) arugula, packed

5½ oz (155 g) Prima Donna cheese

3 cloves garlic

1 cup (250 ml) extra-virgin olive oil

Fine sea salt and freshly ground pepper

1. Place the cashews in an ungreased nonstick pan over medium heat. Toast on the stovetop for 2 to 3 minutes or until light brown, stirring constantly. Keep your eyes on them so they don't burn. Once they're toasted, immediately transfer the cashews to a bowl to stop the cooking process.
2. Meanwhile, gently wash and drain the arugula. Tear the leaves into small pieces and remove the thicker stems. Set aside.
3. Cut the Prima Donna cheese into medium-sized cubes. Set aside.
4. Peel and grate the cloves of garlic.
5. Place the cashews, arugula, Prima Donna cheese, and garlic in a food processor. Mix well, gradually adding the olive oil. Season to taste with salt and pepper.
6. Use the pesto immediately or transfer to an airtight container and keep refrigerated for up to 7 days. Pesto works great as a pasta sauce, used as a dip, or spread on a sandwich.

CHEESE:
Prima Donna

I will never forget the first time I was introduced to Prima Donna cheese. It was in 2006, and I was with my dad at the New York Fancy Food Show: a huge international show where suppliers showcase their world-class products. There I was, a hotshot 26-year-old who thought he knew everything about cheese. Well, let's just say I needed to eat some humble pie, and I did that day. We started in the Dutch cheese section (it was divided into countries), and right away I saw a cheese I had never tried before. After hearing from the presenter that this cheese—Prima Donna—was better than Parmigiano-Reggiano, I decided to try it for myself. It blew my mind. I wouldn't necessarily say it's better than the Italian classic, but it's great in pesto. Hats off to the Vandersterre Groep in the Netherlands for producing such an awesome cheese!

LOW RISK,
HIGH REWARD

178   Mark McEwan Sipping on Gin and Juice

183   Ode to L'Arpège

184   Beemster and Friends

187   The Boss

188   Cacio e Pepe Popcorn

191   Cheese and Crackers Bruce Wayne–Style

192   Drunken Goat in a Pot

195   Époisses by Bob Blumer

196   The Sandwich Roll-Up

199   This Cheese Stands Alone (Part 2 of 2)

Mark McEwan Sipping on
Gin and Juice

PREP	5 minutes
CHILL	4 hours
SERVES	1

1 tsp (5 ml) fine sea salt

2 tsp (10 ml) sugar

1 sprig fresh mint

6 juniper berries

1 lime

1 oz (30 ml) gin

Ice

1 cup (250 ml) tonic, flat

3 thin slices cucumber

7 oz (200 g) chabichou goat cheese (see note)

1. In the bottom of a small mason jar, muddle the salt and sugar with the mint and berries, until the berries are lightly crushed.
2. Cut the lime in half, and cut 1 of the halves into quarters. Add the 2 quarters to the mason jar, and muddle to squeeze out the juices and bruise the lime skins. Remove and discard the lime once you have muddled it. This will cut down on any excess bitterness.
3. Pour the gin into the jar, seal, and shake vigorously to dissolve the salt and sugar. Refrigerate for a minimum of 4 hours, and up to 24 hours.
4. To serve the drink, fill a highball glass with ice and pour the gin mixture overtop. Finish with tonic water and garnish with cucumber slices. Enjoy with small bites of chabichou goat cheese.

My favorite cocktail recipe inspiration comes from one of my mentors, Chef Mark McEwan, and Mr. Gangster Rap himself, Snoop Doggy Dogg. McEwan my words (see what I did there?), this simple pairing will blow away the competition. A special shout-out for this recipe has to go to Mimsey Field, who works at Cheese Boutique and is a wizard with cocktails. Let's just call her Dr. Dre, shall we?

If you can't find chabichou goat cheese from the Loire Valley, ask your cheesemonger for the best creamy goat cheese they have. I chose this one because it's Chef McEwan's favorite.

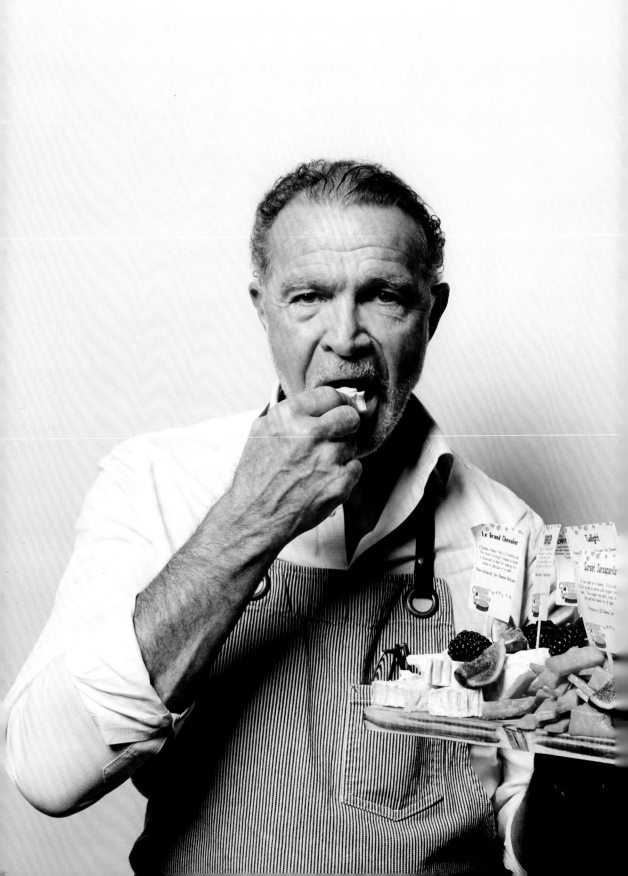

Ode to L'Arpège

PREP	A really fast minute
COOK	N/A
SERVES	2 deserving people

9 oz (255 g) square piece of Comté cheese, room temperature
0.4–0.5 oz (12–15 g) fresh black truffles, shaved

Comté is a cheese near and dear to my heart. Now, I can't take all the credit for the following recipe, as it's a dish I had at a restaurant called L'Arpège in Paris, owned by Alain Passard. The restaurant is 30 years old and has 3 Michelin stars and many global distinctions—this is the Tom Brady of restaurants (minus the Deflategate disaster). This simple pairing makes a colossal impact—French Comté cheese and fresh black truffles.

1. Place the Comté cheese flat on a plate. Cover the cheese in black truffles. (Store your remaining truffles in 1 of 2 ways: covered in uncooked rice—cook the rice later to make a truffle-infused risotto—or wrapped in a dry paper towel with wax paper overtop.)
2. Pour yourself the best French red wine possible. Bordeaux would be ideal.
3. Enjoy the heck out of this.

When you go to buy Comté, taste it first, and make sure it's cut from the freshest possible wheel, as fridge-burnt Comté is the worst thing to taste ever. Truffles are becoming more readily available, but you will still need to go to a high-end specialty store, as a regular grocery store won't carry them. Freshness and quality are key here. Ask where the truffles came from and how fresh they are. If you hear anything other than "France," "Italy," "Croatia," or "Australia" and "less than 4 days old," don't make this recipe. Be patient and wait for the good, fresh stuff to come.

Beemster **and Friends**

PREP   5 minutes
COOK   N/A
SERVES 2–4

9 oz (255 g) beemster extra-old cheese, room temperature
1 piece fresh honeycomb (can be found at a specialty or health
    food store, or some wineries)
1¾ oz (50 g) dark chocolate, chilled
1 loaf of your favorite fruit and nut bread, sliced ½ inch (1.2 cm)
    thick and toasted

1. Carefully cut the rind off the beemster cheese, and shave the
   cheese with a vegetable peeler. Work slowly, and aim for super-
   thin shavings—they work best for this recipe.
2. Place the cheese shavings in the center of your serving vessel
   (something nice please; get fancy). Put a couple of heaping
   spoonfuls of honeycomb anywhere on the plate. Put the
   toasted bread anywhere on the plate. (Are you making it look
   nice? I hope so. These are some worthy ingredients.) Take the
   chilled chocolate and rasp or grate it onto the cheese. The trick
   here is to get the cheese, honeycomb, chocolate, and toasted
   bread all in 1 bite.

CHEESE:
Beemster

In June 2016, a few chef
friends and I took over the
kitchen at Hockley Valley Resort
to create a cheese-focused
tasting menu for a sold-out
crowd of 80 hungry people. I
don't expect you to recreate a
3-hour dinner, so we'll skip the
main courses, but I'll walk you
through the dessert I
created—a simple cheese
course.

I remember my dad telling me stories of when he had to drive to Montreal, Quebec, in the early 70s to buy Brie de Meaux from their markets. At that time, a lot of the great imported cheeses from Europe landed in Montreal and weren't distributed throughout the rest of Canada. My dad knew how wonderful Brie de Meaux was, and he knew he had to stock it at Cheese Boutique, no matter how hard he had to work to get that product. "For the love of food," my dad always says. Speaking as a cheese lover and a cheesemonger, I've seen first hand the impact my father has made on the cheese community nationally. This book wouldn't exist without his hard work and dedication through all these years. Thanks for introducing Brie de Meaux to me, Dad. This recipe is dedicated to you, your love of Brie de Meaux, and your love of apples.

The Boss

PREP	10 minutes
COOK	10 minutes
SERVES	4

4 medium royal gala apples (or any other crisp apple that you enjoy)
5½ oz (155 g) Brie de Meaux cheese, rind cut off and cubed
¼ cup (60 ml) unsalted butter, divided into 4 equal pieces
½ cup (125 ml) chopped walnuts
¼ cup (60 ml) dried cranberries
½ cup (125 ml) Calvados or any other brandy or cognac-type liqueur

1. Preheat the oven to 250°F (120°C).
2. Carefully cut the tops off each apple, and remove the core, about three-quarters down from the top. Take away the heart and the pits, but leave the bottom of the apple intact.
3. Mix the Brie de Meaux cubes with the butter, walnuts, and cranberries. Fill the apples with the Brie de Meaux mixture. Pour in the liqueur. (Don't spill any. Dad will be pissed.)
4. Place the apples on a baking tray, and bake for 10 minutes or until softened and turning golden brown.
5. Serve with a green salad.

Cacio e Pepe Popcorn

PREP   2–3 minutes
COOK   2 more minutes
SERVES   2

½ cup (125 ml) popcorn kernels
¼ cup (60 ml) or a good-sized hunk of unsalted butter
3½ oz (100 g) grated pecorino romano cheese
Freshly ground pepper

1. Place the popcorn kernels into your popcorn maker (I'm sure you have one hiding somewhere, probably beside the fondue pot you never use . . .), and pop away.
2. If you do not have a popcorn maker, heat 1 tablespoon (15 ml) of canola oil in a deep pot over medium-high heat. Place 3 or 4 kernels in the bottom of the pot, and cover with a lid. When those kernels pop, place the rest of the kernels in an even layer on the bottom of the pot, and cover with the lid.
3. Remove the pot from the heat, keeping covered, for about 30 seconds to even out the temperature of the oil, and then return the pot to the heat source.
4. Gently shake the pot over the burner as the popcorn pops.
5. Try to keep the lid ajar to allow the steam to escape, which will keep the popcorn drier and crisper.
6. Once the popping slows down, remove the pot from the heat completely, remove the lid, and immediately dump the popcorn into a bowl so it does not burn.
7. In a small saucepan, melt the butter over medium heat.
8. Divide the popcorn in 2 bowls, and divide the melted butter equally among each. Divide the pecorino romano cheese equally, and garnish each bowl with a few turns of pepper. Gently toss and enjoy this cheesy popcorn with your favorite movie (my favorite is *Gangs of New York*, just in case you were wondering—Leo rules).

CHEESE:
Pecorino Romano

This cheese is known as some of the world's best, but it's not as simple as you might think. If you were to walk into a cheese store and simply ask for a pecorino, it would be like walking into a car dealership and asking for a car. Just as a car sales person would ask you what kind of car you want, your cheesemonger will ask what kind of pecorino you want, too. This recipe is easy and uses a type of pecorino that you'll be able to find almost anywhere—pecorino romano.

There are many different types of pecorino available to buy. Here are just a few of my favorites:
- *Pecorino stagionato: aged pecorino*
- *Pecorino ubriaco: pecorino aged in wine ("ubriaco" means drunk in Italian)*
- *Pecorino affienato: pecorino aged in hay*
- *Pecorino tartufo: pecorino infused with black truffles*
- *Pecorino fresco: fresh pecorino, usually aged only 60 days*
- *Pecorino Toscano: pecorino strictly made in Tuscany (where some of the best stuff comes from)*

CHEESE:
Cashel Blue

This recipe is extremely straightforward but with a huge impact. Celery and blue cheese go so well together, so when you infuse a cracker with celery, it wants—and needs—to be smothered in blue cheese.

Cheese and Crackers
Bruce Wayne–Style

PREP	45 seconds or less
COOK	N/A
SERVES	Best part, it serves as many as you like

1 box (5.3 oz/150 g) celery crackers from the Fine Cheese Co.

9 oz (255 g) Cashel Blue cheese

1 bottle of the best vintage port wine

1. Open the cracker box.
2. Place some cheese on a cracker. Eat that cracker.
3. Sip some wine.
4. Repeat.
5. You're welcome.

Drunken Goat **in a Pot**

PREP   5 minutes plus 30 minutes chilling time and 1 hour
         resting time

COOK   N/A

SERVES   4–6

CHEESE:
**Goat
Cheddar**

9 oz (255 g) goat cheddar cheese, cubed

⅓ cup (85 ml) unsalted butter, softened

Pinch of smoked paprika

¼ cup (60 ml) port, sherry, or Madeira wine

¼ cup (60 ml) roasted and chopped walnuts

4 whole walnuts, halved

While this recipe seems simple, it's even simpler than it appears. It's also a huge crowd-pleaser, especially during the cold-weather holidays.

1. Mix the cheese and the butter together in a food processor to make a smooth paste. Add the paprika and port.
2. Transfer the paste to a small bowl, and add the chopped walnuts. Stir to combine. Transfer the cheese paste to a small decorative pot, and decorate it with the walnut halves on top. Cover with aluminum foil, and refrigerate for 30 minutes to let the flavors come together.
3. Remove the potted cheese from the refrigerator at least 1 hour before serving to allow it to come to room temperature.
4. If you wish to keep your potted cheese for a few days, cover the top with softened unsalted butter. The fat in the butter keeps the dip from drying out. Then cover with aluminum foil, and keep in the refrigerator for up to 7 days.
5. I suggest you enjoy this super-tasty snack with veggie sticks or your favorite crackers.

CHEESE:
Époisses

Époisses **by Bob Blumer**

PREP	1–2 days resting time
COOK	N/A
SERVES	2–4

1 piece Époisses
1 box of your favorite fruit and nut crostini
1 bottle (750 ml) Sauternes wine (or another botrytis-affected late-harvest wine, ice wine, or ice cider)

When I asked Bob Blumer to contribute a recipe, he chose one of the most controversial cheeses ever and came up with the most poetic introduction any cookbook has ever seen:

To the uninitiated, Époisses may seem more threatening than appealing. Its funky barnyard aroma (best described as dirty socks meet sweaty armpits) makes it instantly clear why it is banned from public transport in France. Yes, in France—a country whose tolerance for stinky cheese is legendary. Not unlike the acquired taste of its kindred spirit, the spike-covered durian fruit, Époisses offers the ultimate of pleasures for the adventurous eater who dares to penetrate the force field of its olfactory defenses. Once inside, a liquid of unparalleled flavor oozes, enveloping the palate with a robust, tangy fusion of sweet honey and hay flavors—all culminating in a spine-tingling gastrogasm. The true Époisses experience only comes to those who wait. What follows is my recipe for celebrating it in all its glory.

1. Set the Époisses round, in its unassuming wooden box, out on the counter at room temperature for a minimum of 1 day, but 2 days is ideal. Pass by it occasionally, but don't linger so long as to distract it from its metamorphosis from a solid mass into a puddle of pleasure.
2. When the cheese's brandy-bathed rind begins to shimmer, break the soft, rippled surface of the rind with a spoon. Liberate the gooey interior from its confines, and watch, mesmerized, as the oozing cheese slowly fills in the void left by the divot of the spoon.
3. Spread generously onto the crostini.
4. Take your first bite and luxuriate in the life-affirming layers of flavor as they explode in your mouth. Marvel momentarily at the fact that it tastes nothing like it smells, and how it is unlike any other first taste sensation you have ever experienced.
5. As the flavors linger in your mouth (and believe me, they will), compound your pleasure quotient with a generous sip of dessert wine. Close your eyes and focus on how the sweetness and acidity of the wine act as the perfect foil to the richness of the cheese.
6. Remind yourself that life doesn't get any better.
7. Repeat as necessary.
8. Make sure to finish the cheese or it will stink up the whole house. Take one for the team.

The Sandwich **Roll-Up**

PREP   10 minutes
COOK   3 minutes
SERVES   4

4 slices whole wheat bread
4 tsp (20 ml) basil pesto, divided
8 thin slices emmental cheese (Swiss or local)
4 slices black forest ham (the scariest ham in all the land)

1. Preheat the oven to 300°F (150°C).
2. Remove the crust from each bread slice and flatten the bread with your hands or a rolling pin (I use my hands, but it's your call). Spread 1 teaspoon (5 ml) of basil pesto all over each of the bread slices, and top each with a slice of emmental cheese and then a slice of ham.
3. Turn the stacked bread over, so the ham is face down, and roll up the bread with the ham toward the outside. Secure with a toothpick or skewer.
4. Put the skewered sandwiches on a baking sheet, and warm them in the preheated oven for 2 to 3 minutes or until you see melted emmental coming out the ends of the roll-ups.
5. Have a Toblerone for dessert, like the good ol' days.

**CHEESE:
Emmental**

I remember hating emmental when I was a kid. I found it a bit too stinky, but after years of training, my father finally changed my impression of it. He started us young—whenever my 3 brothers or I would ask for a treat from the store, he ignored our requests for a Toblerone bar, and brought us home cheese instead. He trained our palates in the wonderful world of cheese and told us stories about each one. I remember emmental sticking out from the crowd because of its flavor, but now, it's my ultimate sandwich cheese— nutty, buttery, and complex. Thanks, Dad.

This Cheese Stands Alone (Part 2 of 2)

In 1877, provolone was born in Naples, Italy, and in 1900, a new dairy called Auricchio (named after the family who created it) opened in northern Italy in the town of Cremona.

I'm not talking about the sliced provolone we put in our mortadella sandwiches, I'm talking about top-quality, very complex, very aged Auricchio Provolone—one of the most important cheeses and dairies in Italy. They come in all shapes and sizes, from 50- to 300-pound (25–135 kg) torpedo-shaped cheeses to a 100-pound (45 kg) massive ball-like shape. We have a few of each hanging in our cheese cave.

It was November of 2005, and I was working at a high-end Scotch tasting. The organizers hired Cheese Boutique to curate a cheese station to serve delicious cheeses with all these beautiful Scotches. It was just my dad and me working together; in fact, it was one of the very last events my father worked. We chose what we thought was the perfect cheese to serve with every kind of Scotch: 5-year-old Auricchio Provolone (aged in our cheese cave at the shop).

My father and I have worked hundreds of events like this, so it wasn't anything new. Our setup was easy: a huge 300-pound (135 kg) cheese and good bread. It was enough cheese for 5,000 people, and the event was for 450 people. Everyone attending had a crazily expensive Scotch in their hand, and they were hungry. They came in waves, and one after another, each person was blown away by the simple combination of great Scotch and aged Auricchio Provolone.

Then the crowds died down. It was toward the end of the night, and I saw my father talking with some customers in the corner of the room. I was in command of the provolone now. A man came up to the station on his own. I placed a big hunk of cheese on his plate and explained the cheese to him. He didn't say a word and walked away. About 3 minutes later, a group of a dozen men came charging over to our cheese station, clearly on a mission. The man who had come earlier was at the head of the charge. He was a member of the Auricchio cheese family direct from Italy. What were the odds of me serving his family's cheese to him, 5 years after it was made? He was freaking out. He and his friends kept telling me that they had never tried their cheese like that before, with the complexity and aging, and they couldn't believe how well it went with the Scotch. He was so impressed with how we aged and maintained his family cheese (their dairy has been around for almost 120 years) that he wouldn't leave me alone. I was his best friend, and I think he thought I could walk on water (trust me, I can barely walk and chew gum at the same time). It was a great, successful night, one my father and I will never forget.

The night ended with me struggling to wrap up and put away that monster of a cheese with still so much left over. My father was talking with the Italian cheese makers and they ended the night with what looked like a very important handshake and hug.

Some time later, we received a call from Italy. The Auricchio family were so impressed with the cheese they had at the Scotch tasting that they wanted to make Cheese Boutique a gift. All my father told me was, "There's a huge gift coming for you from Italy." He said this with a big grin on his face. As you'll know from page 126, the gift was a 900-pound (400 kg) torpedo of provolone, which you can still see in Cheese Boutique today.

This recipe, if you want to call it that, makes the perfect dessert or best snack of all time. Try it both ways; you will not be disappointed.

Continued over

PREP	However long it takes you to drive to your cheese shop and back
COOK	None
SERVES	That's up to you (how big a hunk are you buying?)

CHEESE: Auricchio Provolone

As big a piece of aged Auricchio Provolone cheese as your little heart desires

1 bottle of a wicked Scotch (how about Macallan 12, 18, or 25 years—come on, you deserve it)

1. Eat the cheese by chewing and swallowing.
2. Sip the Scotch, savor for a moment, and then swallow.
3. Repeat 100 times (no judgment here).

My best friend, Henry.

Acknowledgments

It's been a long journey for me to write this book, and I've had a blast creating cheesy recipes, telling my family story, and spreading the word about my absolute favorite ingredient of all time, CHEESE. I want to thank everyone who has supported and helped me throughout this long and sometimes grueling, yet fun, process.

Thank you to the entire team at Appetite by Random House for giving me this opportunity. I still can't believe I'm an author, and I hope I made you proud. Zoe Maslow, you are the best editor of all time. I hope Penguin Random House Canada feels as lucky as I do to work with you. Robert McCullough, my publisher, was one of the first people to believe in this book. Thank you for your faith in me. Scott Richardson, the design wiz, thank you for thinking outside the box and for making such a beautiful book. You've been a customer at the shop for a long time, and I'm honored that you wanted to be a part of this project.

Steven and Paula Elphick, and Julie Zambonelli, thank you for all the photography and for making my recipes look incredible. You went above and beyond in every way. Thank you to Blair and Julio Lucas, for making my superhero dreams come true.

Marian and Sean from Branding and Buzzing, without you, I would have never been introduced to Robert and Zoe. I will never forget our Boston trip.

Jordie McTavish, thank you for keeping me organized, calm, and collected when I needed to be.

Thank you to all my colleagues in the food industry across North America who have helped me become the best cheesemonger and business man I can be. To the chefs who graciously provided recipes for this book, I am so grateful for your friendship and your generosity. Thank you, too, to Marc Thuet, Grant van Gameren, Victor Barry, Keith Froggett, Lynn Crawford, Basilio Pesce, Lora Kirk, Porchetta Nick, Alida Soloman, Rob Rossi, Devin Connell, Ivana Raca, Chris Zielinski, John Horne, James Chatto, the entire Langdon Hall family, Chris Nuttall-Smith, Nadège Nourian, Bertrand Alépée, Geoff Hopgood, the Canadian Opera Company, and many more.

Thank you to all the Cheese Boutique staff from the last fifty years. Our store doesn't thrive without your hard work and dedication. Joy Caliva, my right-hand man, you are the Robin to my Batman. Marta Murga, Celina Jagiello, Sadeta Music, and Ralph Newmeister: the four of you have not only taught me so much about cheese and life, but you helped raise me. I love you. Alex Eidelman, our art director and my dear friend, thank you for sharing your unique vision for this cookbook and for always being there for both technical and emotional support.

Thank you to the city of Toronto, and Canada as a whole. You gave my family an opportunity to succeed and have been so good to us. I'm a proud Canadian with deep European roots, and you allowed a humble, hardworking family the chance to make a living and, at the same time, help shape how we eat cheese in our great, bountiful country.

To all my suppliers and the great cheese makers within Canada and abroad, thank you for giving me the tools to sell the best products possible. And a special thank you to the Swiss Cheese Association, Tree of Life, Agropur, JK Overweel, and the International Cheese Company for your constant support.

To Henry and Charlie, my two rescue pups. You both got me through a very hard time in my life. The sweetest dogs ever.

To Batman, thank you for fighting justice and for giving me some of the greatest non-food memories of my life.

To the entire Pristine family (past and present), I wish I had another few chapters to write about what you mean to me and to thank you for all you've done for me over the last thirty-eight years.

And lastly, this cookbook doesn't happen without the four most important people in my life.

Sophia Pristine, you've kept me in line for the last twenty-five years. I've never considered you a sister-in-law, but a sister. I love you and trust you very much, so much so that you are officially my emergency contact for everything in life.

Agim Pristine, my eldest brother, my mentor, and the absolute hardest-working man I've ever met. I am nothing without you; you have been the vision for Cheese Boutique for the last twenty years and I'm so lucky to have been working by your side for all this time. You are the best big brother and business partner anyone could hope for. I know I don't tell you enough, but you are my rock and I love you more than I can say.

Mom and Dad, the two sweetest, most selfless, dedicated, and loving people I know. There are no words to describe what you mean to me and no words to express my gratitude for everything you've done for me. Absolutely everything I do in life is to make you proud because you deserve the best I have to give. I hope to always honor your names and I hope I've made you proud with this book. Dad, I hope to always be your "golden boy" 'cause you will always be my Lion. I will never forget the life lessons you taught me, and are still teaching me. Mom, you were the first person I ever cooked with. I'll never forget cooking and listening to Rick Astley with you in the kitchen. I love you both.

Index

A

Abbot's Gold Caramelised Onion Cheddar
about, 28
in Monty Python Burger, 121
Afrim Is Cuckoo for Kaltbach, 160
aging, buying, and storing cheese, 12–14
Agostino, Rocco (Libretto Croque Pizza), 112–14
alcohol and cheese pairings
beer, 17
Champagne, 163
gin, 178
port, 17, 191
Scotch, 199–200
sherry, 17
wine, 17, 117, 160, 163, 183, 191, 195
almonds
in Creamy Fromage and Biscotti, 163
Marcona, in Burrata Salad, 63
in You Will Make Friends with This Salad, 95
amaretti cookies, in G.O.A.T. (Greatest of All Time), 140–41
anchovies, in Handmade Fusilli with Clams and Broccoli, 110–11
Appenzeller cheese
about, 30
in Embrace the Stinky Bread, 164
appetizers. See cocktails; snacks and appetizers
apple jelly, in "How Do You Like D'em Apples" Bars, 167
apple(s). See also apple jelly
in The Boss, 187
in I Wish I Was at the Cottage Cheese Danish, 40
in You Will Make Friends with This Salad, 95
Applewood cheddar cheese
about, 31
in "How Do You Like D'em Apples" Bars, 167
apricots, in Creamy Fromage and Biscotti, 163
Aprile, Claudio (Bufala with Poached Pears and Toasted Pine Nuts), 60–61
arugula
in Burrata Salad, 63
in My Ode to Stella Pristine Norwegian Corn Cakes, 75
in Niagara Summer Salad, 55

in You Will Make Friends with This Salad, 95
in "You're So Vain" Pesto, 174
ash rind goat cheese, in Niagara Summer Salad, 55
asiago cheese
about, 27
in Cauliflower Asiago Gratin, 105
in Death by Pasta, 103
in Melted Cheese and Pasta a.k.a. Mac and Cheese, 118
Auricchio Provolone cheese
about, 23, 32
in Not So French Onion Soup, 126–27
in This Cheese Stands Alone, 199–200
avocado(s)
in Big Shot East Coast Lobster Rolls, 59
in Slam-Dunk Sandwich, 72

B

bacon, in Slam-Dunk Sandwich, 72
Baked Pasta Quebecois-Style, 99
bananas, in Ardiana Grilled Cheese, 158
Bangerter, Jason (Truffle Soup with Savory Comté Shortbread), 86–87
basil, fresh
in Baked Pasta Quebecois-Style, 99
in Bufala with Poached Pears and Toasted Pine Nuts, 60–61
in Burrata Salad, 63
in Fruity, Cheesy Gazpacho, Por Favor, 161
pesto, in Sandwich Roll-Up, 196
in This Quiche Doesn't Stink, 134–35
in Tomato Pie, 85
beans. See black beans, in Oaxaca Bake; kidney beans
béchamel sauce, 114
beef
in Monty Python Burger, 121
in My Mom's Meatloaf, 122–23
in No-Alarm Chili, 125
in Rock and Roll Grilled Cheese, 82
beemster cheese
about, 31
in Beemster and Friends, 184
beer
and cheese pairing, 17
in Fondue à la Pristine, 115
beets
in Warm Salad of Winter Radish, 90–91

in You Will Make Friends with This Salad, 95
Bell, Ned (Dungeness Crab, White Cheddar, Truffle, and Lime Mac 'n' Cheese), 104
bell peppers
in Don't Mess with Texas Eggs, 39
in Fruity, Cheesy Gazpacho, Por Favor, 161
in My Ode to Stella Pristine Norwegian Corn Cakes, 75
Big Shot East Coast Lobster Rolls, 59
black beans, in Oaxaca Bake, 129
blue cheese. See also Cashel Blue cheese; Roquefort blue cheese; stilton cheese
and alcohol pairings, 17, 191
Blumer, Bob (Époisses), 195
bocconcini cheese. See also Santa Lucia cherry bocconcini cheese
in Death by Pasta, 103
in This Quiche Doesn't Stink, 134–35
boerenkaas cheese
about, 22
in 7 a.m. Pizza, 36
Boss, The, 187
Boulud, Daniel (Stuffed Cheese Pumpkin with Black Rice, Mushrooms, and Cheese), 132–33
brandy, in The Boss, 187
Bread, Embrace the Stinky, 164
breakfast
Don't Mess with Texas Eggs, 39
I Wish I Was at the Cottage Cheese Danish, 40
Most Expensive Eggs Ever, 43
Ricotta and Raspberry Sitting in a Tree..., 45
7 a.m. Pizza, 36
Stefano's Pecorino Fresco Pancakes, 46
Tortillas à la Marta, 49
Wookey and Waffles, 50
brie cheese. See also Brie de Meaux cheese; Brie L'Extra cheese
in Creamy Fromage and Biscotti, 163
Brie de Meaux cheese
about, 31
in The Boss, 187
Brie L'Extra cheese
about, 25
in Peaches and Brie Grilled Cheese, 76

Brillat-Savarin cheese
about, 29
with Fresh Strawberries, 138
broccoli
Handmade Fusilli with, and Clams, 110–11
in Melted Cheese and Pasta a.k.a. Mac and Cheese, 118
in World's Best Frittata, 92
Bufala with Poached Pears and Toasted Pine Nuts, 60–61
Burger, Monty Python, 121
burrata cheese
about, 24
in Burrata Salad, 63
buttermilk
in 1, 2, 3 Strikes You're Out Muffins, 157
in Wookey and Waffles, 50
buying, storing, and aging cheese, 12–14

C
Cacio e Pepe Popcorn, 188
Cake, Olive Oil and Pistachio, 146–48
Cannoli, Deconstructed, 142
Capra, Massimo (Polenta Arancini), 170–71
Caramel Sauce, 143
Caramelized Onions, 114. See also Abbot's Gold Caramelised Onion Cheddar
carrots
in Most Delicious Spanish Rice Ever, 64
in You Will Make Friends with This Salad, 95
Cashel Blue cheese
about, 32
in Cheese and Crackers Bruce Wayne–Style, 191
cashew nuts, in "You're So Vain" Pesto, 174
Casserole, Seafood, 130–31
cauliflower
Asiago Gratin, 105
in Dungeness Crab, White Cheddar, Truffle, and Lime Mac 'n' Cheese, 104
in Niagara Summer Salad, 55
celery crackers, in Cheese and Crackers Bruce Wayne–Style, 191
chabichou goat cheese
about, 26
with Gin and Juice, 178
Champagne and cheese pairing, 163
cheddar cheese. See also Abbot's Gold Caramelised Onion

Cheddar; Applewood cheddar cheese; Wookey Hole cheddar cheese
aged, in Melted Cheese and Pasta a.k.a. Mac and Cheese, 118
and alcohol pairing, 17
Canadian, in Tomato Pie, 85
goat, in Drunken Goat in a Pot, 192
white, and Dungeness Crab, Truffle, and Lime Mac 'n' Cheese, 104
Cheese and Crackers Bruce Wayne–Style, 191
cheese 101
and alcohol pairings. See alcohol and cheese pairings
buying, storing, and aging, 12–14
cheese in various parts of the world, 15–16
constructing a cheese platter, 16–17
milk types, 14
pasteurized versus unpasteurized, 15
seasons, 12
Cheese Pumpkin Stuffed with Black Rice, Mushrooms, and Cheese, 132–33
cheesecake, 140–41
cherry(ies), in Fruity, Cheesy Gazpacho, Por Favor, 161. See also Santa Lucia cherry bocconcini cheese
Chèvre des Alpes goat cheese
about, 29
in G.O.A.T. (Greatest of All Time), 140–41
chicken
Crispy, Schwarzenegger-Style, 100
in Manchego Duero Paella Barbecue-Style, 117
Chili, No-Alarm, 125
chili-gouda cheese, in Slam-Dunk Sandwich, 72
chocolate
dark, in Beemster and Friends, 184
dark, in Deconstructed Cannoli, 142
milk or dark, in Ardiana Grilled Cheese, 158
white, in G.O.A.T. (Greatest of All Time), 140–41
cilantro, fresh
in Embrace the Stinky Bread, 164
in Most Delicious Spanish Rice Ever, 64
in Oaxaca Bake, 129
Clams and Broccoli, Handmade Fusilli with, 110–11

cocktails. See also alcohol and cheese pairings
Mark McEwan Sipping on Gin and Juice, 178
cognac, in The Boss, 187
Comté cheese
about, 25
in Ode to L'Arpège, 183
in Savory Comté Shortbread, 87
Cookies, "I'm Not Afraid of Blue Cheese Anymore" Caramelized, 143
corn, in Oaxaca Bake, 129. See also cornmeal or corn flour
cornmeal or corn flour
in My Ode to Stella Pristine Norwegian Corn Cakes, 75
in Olive Oil and Pistachio Cake, 146
in Polenta Arancini, 170–71
in Tortillas à la Marta
cotija cheese
about, 30
in Fruity, Cheesy Gazpacho, Por Favor, 161
cottage cheese
about, 22
Danish, I Wish I Was at the, 40
couscous, in My Mom's Meatloaf, 122–23
cow's milk cheese, about, 14. See also specific types
crab
Dungeness, and White Cheddar, Truffle, and Lime Mac 'n' Cheese, 104
in Seafood Casserole, 130–31
Crackers and Cheese Bruce Wayne–Style, 191
cranberries, in The Boss, 187
cream cheese
about, 30
in Matty's Game Day Dip, 168
in X-Men Ice Cream, 152
Creamy Fromage and Biscotti, 163
crème fraiche, in Relax Napoleon, It's Just Goat Cheese Dumplings, 80–81
Crispy Chicken Schwarzenegger-Style, 100
Crunchy Meringue, 147–48
cucumber(s)
in Mark McEwan Sipping on Gin and Juice, 178
in Stella Salad, 56

D
Danish, I Wish I Was at the Cottage Cheese, 40
dates, in Slam-Dunk Sandwich, 72

Death by Pasta, 103
Deconstructed Cannoli, 142
DeMontis, Rita (Seafood Casserole), 130–31
dessert
    Brillat-Savarin with Fresh Strawberries, 138
    Deconstructed Cannoli, 142
    G.O.A.T. (Greatest of All Time), 140–41
    Grilled Pineapple with Mascarpone, 144
    "I'm Not Afraid of Blue Cheese Anymore" Caramelized Cookies, 143
    Olive Oil and Pistachio Cake, 146–48
    Reggiano the Mighty, 151
    X-Men Ice Cream, 152
dill, fresh, in Big Shot East Coast Lobster Rolls, 59
dinner
    Baked Pasta Quebecois-Style, 99
    Cauliflower Asiago Gratin, 105
    Crispy Chicken Schwarzenegger-Style, 100
    Death by Pasta, 103
    Dungeness Crab, White Cheddar, Truffle, and Lime Mac 'n' Cheese, 104
    Dynamic Duo, 107
    Fondue à la Pristine, 115
    Gattò di Patate, 108
    Handmade Fusilli with Clams and Broccoli, 110–11
    Libretto Croque Pizza, 112–14
    Manchego Duero Paella Barbecue-Style, 117
    Melted Cheese and Pasta a.k.a. Mac and Cheese, 118
    Monty Python Burger, 121
    My Mom's Meatloaf, 122–23
    No-Alarm Chili, 125
    Not So French Onion Soup, 126–27
    Oaxaca Bake, 129
    Seafood Casserole, 130–31
    Stuffed Cheese Pumpkin with Black Rice, Mushrooms, and Cheese, 132–33
    This Quiche Doesn't Stink, 134–35
Don't Mess with Texas Eggs, 39
Drunken Goat in a Pot, 192
Dumplings, Goat Cheese, 80–81
Dungeness Crab, White Cheddar, Truffle, and Lime Mac 'n' Cheese, 104
Dynamic Duo, 107

E
eggplant, in Baked Pasta Quebecois-Style, 99
eggs
    in Crunchy Meringue, 147–48
    Don't Mess with Texas, 39
    Most Expensive Ever, 43
    in 7 a.m. Pizza, 36
    in This Quiche Doesn't Stink, 134–35
    in World's Best Frittata, 92
Embrace the Stinky Bread, 164
emmental cheese
    about, 27
    in Fondue à la Pristine, 115
    in Rock and Roll Grilled Cheese, 82
    in Sandwich Roll-Up, 196
endive, in Warm Salad of Winter Radish, 90–91
Époisses
    about, 32
    with crostini and wine, 195
escarole, in Warm Salad of Winter Radish, 90–91

F
Fermented Ricotta Gnocchi, 66–68
feta cheese
    about, 23
    in My Mom's Meatloaf, 122–23
    in Stella Salad, 56
figs, in Creamy Fromage and Biscotti, 163
fish, in Seafood Casserole, 130–31
Fondue à la Pristine, 115
fontina cheese
    about, 29
    in Polenta Arancini, 170–71
    in Seafood Casserole, 130–31
    in This Quiche Doesn't Stink, 134–35
Forgione, Michele (Handmade Fusilli with Clams and Broccoli), 110–11
Frittata, World's Best, 92
Fruity, Cheesy Gazpacho, Por Favor, 161

G
Gattò di Patate, 108
Gazpacho, Fruity, Cheesy, Por Favor, 161
Gentile, Rob (Fermented Ricotta Gnocchi), 66–68
Gin and Juice, Mark McEwan Sipping On, 178
ginger, in Crispy Chicken Schwarzenegger-Style, 100

Glengarry Lankaaster cheese
    about, 26
    in World's Best Frittata, 92
Gnocchi, Fermented Ricotta, 66–68
G.O.A.T. (Greatest of All Time), 140–41
goat cheese. See also chabichou goat cheese; Chèvre des Alpes goat cheese; feta cheese; halloumi cheese; Valençay cheese
    about, 14
    ash rind, in Niagara Summer Salad, 55
    goat cheddar, in Drunken Goat in a Pot, 192
    in Very Much Alive Pasta, 89
    whipped, 147
    and wine pairing, 17
Goodyear, Jonathan (Brillat-Savarin with Fresh Strawberries), 138
gouda cheese
    about, 24
    aged, in Oysters Gouda, Hold the Rockefeller, 169
    chili, in Slam-Dunk Sandwich, 72
Grana Padano cheese
    about, 27
    in Dungeness Crab, White Cheddar, Truffle, and Lime Mac 'n' Cheese, 104
Grand Marnier, in Fondue à la Pristine, 115
grilled cheese
    Ardiana, 158
    Peaches and Brie, 76
    Rock and Roll, 82
Grilled Pineapple with Mascarpone, 144
gruyère cheese
    about, 28
    in Fondue à la Pristine, 115
    Kaltbach, Afrim Is Cuckoo for, 160
    in Libretto Croque Pizza, 112–14
    in Stuffed Cheese Pumpkin with Black Rice, Mushrooms, and Cheese, 132–33
    in Tomato Pie, 85
Gushue, Jonathan (Ragusano Soup), 78

H
halloumi cheese
    about, 24
    in Hail Halloumi, 71
    in Warm Salad of Winter Radish, 90–91
ham
    in Libretto Croque Pizza, 112–14
    in Sandwich Roll-Up, 196
    in Wookey and Waffles, 50

Handmade Fusilli with Clams and Broccoli, 110–11
Harding, Craig (Niagara Summer Salad), 55
havarti cheese
    about, 30
    in Ardiana Grilled Cheese, 158
honey. See also honeycomb
    in Bufala with Poached Pears and Toasted Pine Nuts, 60–61
    in Caramelized Onions, 114
    in Poached Rhubarb, 147
    in Ricotta and Raspberry Sitting in a Tree..., 45
    in Whipped Goat Cheese, 147
honeycomb. See also honey
    in Beemster and Friends, 184
"How Do You Like D'em Apples" Bars, 167
Hughes, Chuck (Tomato Pie), 85

I

I Wish I Was at the Cottage Cheese Danish, 40
Ice Cream, X-Men, 152
"I'm Not Afraid of Blue Cheese Anymore" Caramelized Cookies, 143

J

jalapeño peppers
    in Embrace the Stinky Bread, 164
    in Matty's Game Day Dip, 168
Jarlsberg cheese
    about, 25
    in My Ode to Stella Pristine Norwegian Corn Cakes, 75
    in Seafood Casserole, 130–31
juniper berries, in Mark McEwan Sipping on Gin and Juice, 178

K

Kaltbach, Afrim Is Cuckoo for, 160
kidney beans
    in Don't Mess with Texas Eggs, 39
    in No-Alarm Chili, 125
    in Oaxaca Bake, 129
Kirsch, in Fondue à la Pristine, 115

L

lager. See beer
lamb, in Monty Python Burger, 121
leeks, in Truffle Soup, 86–87
lemon balm, fresh, in Warm Salad of Winter Radish, 90–91
lemon stilton cheese
    about, 30
    in 1, 2, 3 Strikes You're Out Muffins, 157

lentils, in Warm Salad of Winter Radish, 90–91
Libretto Croque Pizza, 112–14
lime(s)
    and Dungeness Crab, White Cheddar, and Truffle Mac 'n' Cheese, 104
    in Mark McEwan Sipping on Gin and Juice, 178
lobster(s)
    in Matty's Game Day Dip, 168
    Rolls, Big Shot East Coast, 59
lunch
    Big Shot East Coast Lobster Rolls, 59
    Bufala with Poached Pears and Toasted Pine Nuts, 60–61
    Burrata Salad, 63
    Fermented Ricotta Gnocchi, 66–68
    Hail Halloumi, 71
    Most Delicious Spanish Rice Ever, 64
    My Ode to Stella Pristine Norwegian Corn Cakes, 75
    Niagara Summer Salad, 55
    Peaches and Brie Grilled Cheese, 76
    Ragusano Soup, 78
    Relax Napoleon, It's Just Goat Cheese Dumplings, 80–81
    Rock and Roll Grilled Cheese, 82
    Slam-Dunk Sandwich, 72
    Stella Salad, 56
    Tomato Pie, 85
    Truffle Soup with Savory Comté Shortbread, 86–87
    Very Much Alive Pasta, 89
    Warm Salad of Winter Radish, 90–91
    World's Best Frittata and I Can Prove It, 92
    You Will Make Friends with This Salad, 95

M

Mac and Cheese a.k.a. Melted Cheese and Pasta, 118
Mac 'n' Cheese, Dungeness Crab, White Cheddar, Truffle, and Lime, 104
Madeira
    in Drunken Goat in a Pot, 192
    in Truffle Soup, 86–87
manchego duero cheese
    about, 28
    in Paella Barbecue-Style, 117
maple syrup, in Warm Salad of Winter Radish, 90–91
Marcona almonds, in Burrata Salad, 63

Mark McEwan Sipping on Gin and Juice, 178
Marsala wine, in Deconstructed Cannoli, 142
masa harina (corn flour), in Tortillas à la Marta, 49. See also cornmeal or corn flour
mascarpone cheese
    about, 27
    in Deconstructed Cannoli, 142
    in Dungeness Crab, White Cheddar, Truffle, and Lime Mac 'n' Cheese, 104
    with Grilled Pineapple, 144
Matty's Game Day Dip, 168
Meatballs, Stuffed Turkey, Matt Damon–Style, 173
Meatless Wheatless Pizza, 166
Meatloaf, My Mom's, 122–23
Melted Cheese and Pasta a.k.a. Mac and Cheese, 118
Meringue, Crunchy, 147–48
milk types for cheese, 14, 22–32
mimolette cheese, in X-Men Ice Cream, 152
mint, fresh
    in Mark McEwan Sipping on Gin and Juice, 178
    in Olive Oil and Pistachio Cake, 146–48
    in Stella Salad, 56
Monterey Jack cheese
    about, 22
    in Don't Mess with Texas Eggs, 39
Monty Python Burger, 121
Most Delicious Spanish Rice Ever, 64
Most Expensive Eggs Ever, 43
mozzarella cheese. See also burrata cheese; mozzarella di bufala cheese
    about, 31
    fresh, in Meatless Wheatless Pizza, 166
    in Gattò di Patate, 108
    in Seafood Casserole, 130–31
    in Stuffed Turkey Meatballs Matt Damon–Style, 173
mozzarella di bufala cheese
    about, 24
    in Bufala with Poached Pears and Toasted Pine Nuts, 60–61
Muffins, 1, 2, 3 Strikes You're Out, 157
mushrooms
    button, in Death by Pasta, 103
    button, in Seafood Casserole, 130–31
    cremini, in Dynamic Duo, 107
    cremini, in Polenta Arancini, 170–71

portobello, in Meatless Wheatless Pizza, 166
portobello, in Truffle Soup, 86–87
Stuffed Cheese Pumpkin with Black Rice, Cheese, and, 132–33
in World's Best Frittata, 92
My Mom's Meatloaf, 122–23
My Ode to Stella Pristine Norwegian Corn Cakes, 75

N

Niagara Summer Salad, 55
No-Alarm Chili, 125
Not So French Onion Soup, 126–27
nuts. See specific types

O

oats, in 1, 2, 3 Strikes You're Out Muffins, 157
Oaxaca cheese
about, 29
in Oaxaca Bake, 129
Ode to L'Arpège, 183
Oka cheese. See also Oka L'Artisan cheese
about, 26
in Baked Pasta Quebecois-Style, 99
Oka L'Artisan cheese. See also Oka cheese
about, 26
in Crispy Chicken Schwarzenegger-Style, 100
Olive Oil and Pistachio Cake, 146–48
olives
in Meatless Wheatless Pizza, 166
in Oaxaca Bake, 129
Olson, Michael and Anna (Cauliflower Asiago Gratin), 105
1, 2, 3 Strikes You're Out Muffins, 157
onion(s)
Caramelized, 114. See also Abbot's Gold Caramelised Onion Cheddar
Soup, Not So French, 126–27
orange(s) and juice
in Deconstructed Cannoli, 142
in Grilled Pineapple with Mascarpone, 144
oregano, fresh
in Cauliflower Asiago Gratin, 105
in Stella Salad, 56
Oysters Gouda, Hold the Rockefeller, 169

P

Paella, Manchego Duero, Barbecue-Style, 117

Pancakes, Stefano's Pecorino Fresco, 46
Parmigiano-Reggiano cheese
about, 28
in Cauliflower Asiago Gratin, 105
in Handmade Fusilli with Clams and Broccoli, 110–11
in Libretto Croque Pizza, 112–14
in Polenta Arancini, 170–71
in Reggiano the Mighty, 151
and Ricotta Gnocchi, 67
parsley, fresh
in Death by Pasta, 103
in Matty's Game Day Dip, 168
in No-Alarm Chili, 125
in Seafood Casserole, 130–31
in Warm Salad of Winter Radish, 90–91
pasta
Baked, Quebecois-Style, 99
Death by, 103
Dungeness Crab, White Cheddar, Truffle, and Lime Mac 'n' Cheese, 104
Handmade Fusilli with Clams and Broccoli, 110–11
and Melted Cheese a.k.a. Mac and Cheese, 118
in No-Alarm Chili, 125
Very Much Alive, 89
pasteurized versus unpasteurized cheese, 15
peaches
and Brie Grilled Cheese, 76
in Fruity, Cheesy Gazpacho, Por Favor, 161
in Niagara Summer Salad, 55
Pears, Poached, with Bufala and Pine Nuts, 60–61
peas
in Most Delicious Spanish Rice Ever, 64
in Ragusano Soup, 78
in Seafood Casserole, 130–31
in Warm Salad of Winter Radish, 90–91
pecorino cheese. See also pecorino fresco cheese; truffle pecorino cheese
about, 32, 188
in Cacio e Pepe Popcorn, 188
pecorino fresco cheese
about, 23, 188
in Stefano's Pancakes, 46
peppers. See also bell peppers
jalapeño, in Embrace the Stinky Bread, 164
jalapeño, in Matty's Game Day Dip, 168

serrano, in Most Delicious Spanish Rice Ever, 64
pesto, arugula, "You're So Vain," 174
pesto, basil, in Sandwich Roll-Up, 196
Pettit, Matt Dean (Matty's Game Day Dip), 168
phyllo pastry, in Tomato Pie, 85
Pie, Tomato, 85
pine nuts
in This Quiche Doesn't Stink, 134–35
Toasted, with Bufala and Poached Pears, 60–61
Pineapple, Grilled, with Mascarpone, 144
pistachio(s)
in Brillat-Savarin with Fresh Strawberries, 138
in "How Do You Like D'em Apples" Bars, 167
and Olive Oil Cake, 146–48
pizza
Libretto Croque, 112–14
Meatless Wheatless, 166
7 a.m., 36
Poached Rhubarb, 147
Polenta Arancini, 170–71
Popcorn, Cacio e Pepe, 188
port
with Cheese and Crackers Bruce Wayne–Style, 191
and cheese pairings, 17, 191
in Drunken Goat in a Pot, 192
potatoes
in Dynamic Duo, 107
in Gattò di Patate, 108
hash brown, in 7 a.m. Pizza, 36
in Most Delicious Spanish Rice Ever, 64
Prima Donna cheese
about, 31
in "You're So Vain" Pesto, 174
prosciutto
in Burrata Salad, 63
in Dynamic Duo, 107
provolone cheese. See also Auricchio Provolone cheese
in Fermented Ricotta Gnocchi, 66–68
smoked, in Big Shot East Coast Lobster Rolls, 59
puff pastry, in I Wish I Was at the Cottage Cheese Danish, 40
Pumpkin, Cheese, Stuffed with Black Rice, Mushrooms, and Cheese, 132–33

Q

queso fresco cheese
about, 23
in Tortillas à la Marta, 49
quiche, 134–35
quinoa, in Stella Salad, 56

R

raclette cheese
about, 27
in Dynamic Duo, 107
Radish, Winter, Warm Salad of,
90–91
Ragusano cheese
about, 25
in Gattò di Patate, 108
in Ragusano Soup, 78
raisins, in You Will Make Friends with
This Salad, 95
rapini, in Very Much Alive Pasta, 89
raspberry(ies)
in Fruity, Cheesy Gazpacho, Por
Favor, 161
and Ricotta Sitting in a Tree..., 45
Red Fox cheese
about, 28
in No-Alarm Chili, 125
Reggiano the Mighty, 151
Relax Napoleon, It's Just Goat
Cheese Dumplings, 80–81
Rhubarb, Poached, 147
rice
Black, Stuffed Cheese Pumpkin
with Mushrooms, Cheese,
and, 132–33
in Manchego Duero Paella
Barbecue-Style, 117
in Seafood Casserole, 130–31
Spanish, Most Delicious Ever, 64
Ricotta and Raspberry Sitting in a
Tree..., 45
ricotta cheese. See also Santa Lucia
ricotta cheese
in Deconstructed Cannoli, 142
Gnocchi, Fermented, 66–68
in G.O.A.T. (Greatest of All Time),
140–41
in Matty's Game Day Dip, 168
riesling, with Afrim Is Cuckoo for
Kaltbach, 160
Rock and Roll Grilled Cheese, 82
Roquefort blue cheese
about, 29
in "I'm Not Afraid of Blue Cheese
Anymore" Caramelized
Cookies, 143
rosemary, fresh
in Caramelized Onions, 114
Rosemary Oil, 60–61

S

salad(s)
Burrata, 63
Niagara Summer, 55
Stella, 56
of Winter Radish, Warm, 90–91
You Will Make Friends with This, 95
salami cacciatore, in Gattò di Patate,
108
salsa
in Oaxaca Bake, 129
in Stuffed Turkey Meatballs Matt
Damon–Style, 173
Salsa Verde, 164
sandwich(es)
Ardiana Grilled Cheese, 158
Big Shot East Coast Lobster
Rolls, 59
Peaches and Brie Grilled
Cheese, 76
Rock and Roll Grilled Cheese, 82
Roll-Up, 196
Slam-Dunk, 72
Santa Lucia cherry bocconcini
cheese
about, 26
in You Will Make Friends with This
Salad, 95
Santa Lucia ricotta cheese
about, 22
in Ricotta and Raspberry Sitting in
a Tree..., 45
sausage, in 7 a.m. Pizza, 36
Sauternes with Époisses, 195
Savory Comté Shortbread, 87
scallops, in Seafood Casserole,
130–31
Scotch, with Auricchio Provolone
cheese, 199–200
Seafood Casserole, 130–31
seasons for cheese, 12
serrano peppers, in Most Delicious
Spanish Rice Ever, 64
7 a.m. Pizza, 36
sheep cheese, about, 14. See also
halloumi cheese; manchego
duero cheese; pecorino
cheese; pecorino fresco
cheese; Roquefort blue
cheese; truffle pecorino
cheese; Zamorano cheese
sherry
and cheese pairing, 17
in Drunken Goat in a Pot, 192
in Seafood Casserole, 130–31
shortbread
in "I'm Not Afraid of Blue Cheese
Anymore" Caramelized
Cookies, 143
Savory Comté, 87

shrimp
in Manchego Duero Paella
Barbecue-Style, 117
in Seafood Casserole, 130–31
Slam-Dunk Sandwich, 72
smoked provolone cheese, in Big
Shot East Coast Lobster Rolls,
59
smoothie, Ricotta and Raspberry
Sitting in a Tree..., 45
snacks and appetizers
Afrim Is Cuckoo for Kaltbach, 160
Ardiana Grilled Cheese, 158
Beemster and Friends, 184
Boss, The, 187
Cacio e Pepe Popcorn, 188
Cheese and Crackers Bruce
Wayne–Style, 191
Creamy Fromage and Biscotti,
163
Drunken Goat in a Pot, 192
Embrace the Stinky Bread, 164
Époisses, 195
Fruity, Cheesy Gazpacho, Por
Favor, 161
"How Do You Like D'em Apples"
Bars, 167
Matty's Game Day Dip, 168
Meatless Wheatless Pizza, 166
Ode to L'Arpège, 183
1, 2, 3 Strikes You're Out Muffins,
157
Oysters Gouda, Hold the
Rockefeller, 169
Polenta Arancini, 170–71
Sandwich Roll-Up, 196
Stuffed Turkey Meatballs Matt
Damon–Style, 173
This Cheese Stands Alone, 199–
200
"You're So Vain" Pesto, 174
soup(s)
Not So French Onion, 126–27
Ragusano, 78
Truffle, with Savory Comté
Shortbread, 86–87
Spanish Rice, Most Delicious Ever, 64
spinach
in Big Shot East Coast Lobster
Rolls, 59
in Meatless Wheatless Pizza, 166
in Relax Napoleon, It's Just Goat
Cheese Dumplings, 80–81
in This Quiche Doesn't Stink,
134–35
sprouts, in Warm Salad of Winter
Radish, 90–91
Stefano's Pecorino Fresco Pancakes,
46
Stella Salad, 56

stilton cheese. *See also* lemon stilton cheese
about, 157
and alcohol pairing, 17
storing, buying, and aging cheese, 12–14
strawberry(ies)
Fresh, with Brillat-Savarin, 138
in Fruity, Cheesy Gazpacho, Por Favor, 161
in 1, 2, 3 Strikes You're Out Muffins, 157
in Reggiano the Mighty, 151
Stuffed Cheese Pumpkin with Black Rice, Mushrooms, and Cheese, 132–33
Stuffed Turkey Meatballs Matt Damon–Style, 173
sun-dried tomatoes. *See also* tomatoes or tomato sauce
in Cauliflower Asiago Gratin, 105
in Polenta Arancini, 170–71
Swiss cheese. *See* emmental cheese; gruyère cheese; raclette cheese

T
This Cheese Stands Alone, 199–200
This Quiche Doesn't Stink, 134–35
thyme, fresh
in Fondue à la Pristine, 115
in Melted Cheese and Pasta a.k.a. Mac and Cheese, 118
in Not So French Onion Soup, 126–27
in Peaches and Brie Grilled Cheese, 76
in Relax Napoleon, It's Just Goat Cheese Dumplings, 80–81
in Truffle Soup, 86–87
in Warm Salad of Winter Radish, 90–91
tomatillos, in Embrace the Stinky Bread, 164
tomatoes or tomato sauce. *See also* sun-dried tomatoes
in Baked Pasta Quebecois-Style, 99
in Burrata Salad, 63
in Don't Mess with Texas Eggs, 39
in Hail Halloumi, 71
in Manchego Duero Paella Barbecue-Style, 117
in Meatless Wheatless Pizza, 166
in Melted Cheese and Pasta a.k.a. Mac and Cheese, 118

in Most Delicious Spanish Rice Ever, 64
in My Mom's Meatloaf, 122–23
in No-Alarm Chili, 125
in Oaxaca Bake, 129
in Relax Napoleon, It's Just Goat Cheese Dumplings, 80–81
in Seafood Casserole, 130–31
in Stella Salad, 56
in Stuffed Turkey Meatballs Matt Damon–Style, 173
in This Quiche Doesn't Stink, 134–35
in Tomato Pie, 85
in X-Men Ice Cream, 152
tonic, in Mark McEwan Sipping on Gin and Juice, 178
tortillas
à la Marta, 49
in Oaxaca Bake, 129
Treviso, in Warm Salad of Winter Radish, 90–91
truffle pecorino cheese
about, 22
in Most Expensive Eggs Ever, 43
truffle(s). *See also* truffle pecorino cheese
black, in Fermented Ricotta Gnocchi, 66–68
black, in Ode to L'Arpège, 183
paste, in Dungeness Crab, White Cheddar, Truffle, and Lime Mac 'n' Cheese, 104
Soup with Savory Comté Shortbread, 86–87
turkey
Meatballs, Stuffed, Matt Damon–Style, 173
in Peaches and Brie Grilled Cheese, 76

U
unpasteurized versus pasteurized cheese, 15

V
Valençay cheese
about, 25
in Relax Napoleon, It's Just Goat Cheese Dumplings, 80–81
and wine pairing, 17
vermouth, in Deconstructed Cannoli, 142
Very Much Alive Pasta, 89
Vitiello, Cory (Olive Oil and Pistachio Cake), 146–48

W
walnuts
in The Boss, 187
in Death by Pasta, 103
in Drunken Goat in a Pot, 192
in Stuffed Cheese Pumpkin with Black Rice, Mushrooms, and Cheese, 132–33
Walsh, Anthony (Warm Salad of Winter Radish), 90–91
Warm Salad of Winter Radish, 90–91
water buffalo cheese, about, 14. *See also* burrata cheese; mozzarella di bufala cheese
Whipped Goat Cheese, 147
White Cheddar, Dungeness Crab, Truffle, and Lime Mac 'n' Cheese, 104
white chocolate, in G.O.A.T. (Greatest of All Time), 140–41. *See also* chocolate
wine
and cheese pairings, 17, 117, 160, 163, 183, 191, 195
in Handmade Fusilli with Clams and Broccoli, 110–11
Marsala, in Deconstructed Cannoli, 142
in Not So French Onion Soup, 126–27
Wookey Hole cheddar cheese
about, 23
in Wookey and Waffles, 50
World's Best Frittata and I Can Prove It, 92

X
X-Men Ice Cream, 152

Y
You Will Make Friends with This Salad, 95
"You're So Vain" Pesto, 174

Z
Zamorano cheese
about, 24
in Most Delicious Spanish Rice Ever, 64
zucchini
in Baked Pasta Quebecois-Style, 99
in Manchego Duero Paella Barbecue-Style, 117
in This Quiche Doesn't Stink, 134–35